D0331601

The Responsibility to Defend:
Rethinking Germany's
Strategic Culture

Bastian Giegerich

Maximilian Terhalle

'Appearing just before a historic German election that marks the end of the Merkel era, this excellent and illuminating study by Bastian Giegerich and Maximilian Terhalle could not be more timely. It provides a succinct analysis of the strategic questions besetting Germany and argues forcefully for a more forward-leaning posture.'

– *Dr Constanze Stelzenmüller, Fritz Stern Chair, Center on the United States and Europe, The Brookings Institution*

'Giegerich and Terhalle make a reasoned and urgent appeal for Europe's wealthiest state to take responsibility for defending the Western order in which it has for so long thrived but whose strategic foundations it has often neglected. Any German who believes that things can continue as they are at present should read this book.'

– *A. Wess Mitchell, former US Assistant Secretary of State for Europe*

'This book presents an excellent and comprehensive analysis of the many deficits of current German defence policy. It is a must-read for everyone interested or actively involved in German defence and security policy.'

– *Professor Dr Joachim Krause, Director, Institute for Security Policy at the University of Kiel – ISPK*

'Germany's strategic trajectory remains largely aimless, conceptually, politically and militarily, at a time of growing security challenges. The superbly qualified authors offer a road map to move Germany's security debate from echo-chamber politics to answering the question: what is Germany's power for?'

– *Professor François Heisbourg, Senior Adviser for Europe, IISS*

The Responsibility to Defend:
Rethinking Germany's Strategic Culture

Bastian Giegerich

Maximilian Terhalle

IISS The International Institute for Strategic Studies

The International Institute for Strategic Studies

Arundel House | 6 Temple Place | London | WC2R 2PG | UK

First published June 2021 by **Routledge**
4 Park Square, Milton Park, Abingdon, Oxon, OX14 4RN

for **The International Institute for Strategic Studies**
Arundel House, 6 Temple Place, London, WC2R 2PG, UK
www.iiss.org

Simultaneously published in the USA and Canada by **Routledge**
52 Vanderbilt Avenue, New York, NY 10017

Routledge is an imprint of Taylor & Francis, an Informa Business

© 2021 The International Institute for Strategic Studies

DIRECTOR-GENERAL AND CHIEF EXECUTIVE Dr John Chipman
EDITOR Dr Benjamin Rhode
ASSOCIATE EDITOR Alice Aveson
EDITORIAL Vivien Antwi, Mubasil Chaudhry, Nick Fargher, Jill Lally
COVER/PRODUCTION John Buck, Carolina Vargas, Kelly Verity
COVER IMAGE: Getty

The International Institute for Strategic Studies is an independent centre for research, information and debate on the problems of conflict, however caused, that have, or potentially have, an important military content. The Council and Staff of the Institute are international and its membership is drawn from almost 100 countries. The Institute is independent and it alone decides what activities to conduct. It owes no allegiance to any government, any group of governments or any political or other organisation. The IISS stresses rigorous research with a forward-looking policy orientation and places particular emphasis on bringing new perspectives to the strategic debate.

The Institute's publications are designed to meet the needs of a wider audience than its own membership and are available on subscription, by mail order and in good bookshops. Further details at www.iiss.org.

All rights reserved. No part of this book may be reprinted or reproduced or utilised in any form or by any electronic, mechanical or other means, now known or hereafter invented, including photocopying and recording, or in any information storage or retrieval system, without permission in writing from the publishers.

British Library Cataloguing in Publication Data
A catalogue record for this book is available from the British Library

Library of Congress Cataloging in Publication Data

ADELPHI series
ISSN 1944-5571

ADELPHI 477
ISBN 978-1-032-12273-1

Contents

ACKNOWLEDGEMENTS

The question of Germany's underperformance in security and defence has vexed us as authors for years. In 2016, we worked together on an article for the IISS journal *Survival* exploring the purpose of German power. Thus, in the summer of 2020, when Benjamin Rhode, Editor of the *Adelphi* series, asked whether there might be a book to be written about German security and defence policy at the end of the Merkel era, we did not need much convincing. Ben deserves an extraordinary amount of credit for moving this project along swiftly and for giving it much greater coherence than the draft version had originally. He also produced the title, which we rather like. The Publications team at the IISS worked as fast and professionally as ever on copy-editing, typesetting, layout and design. Dana Allin, John Chipman and Sarah Raine read parts or all of the manuscript and provided many comments that made it better. Douglas Barrie, Nigel Inkster and John Raine helped to improve our assessments in important aspects. We discussed the subject matter of this book with a number of serving and former officials as well as analysts from Germany and partner countries. Their insights were very valuable and informed the book. Our families deserve special thanks for their exceptional support – or, in the case of the children, tolerance – for this project.

INTRODUCTION

Germany, led by Chancellor Angela Merkel from 2005 until 2021, is a country that gets many things right. It weathered the 2008–09 economic crisis better than others. Its citizens enjoy solid economic growth, a high quality of life and strong public services. Even Merkel's perhaps most controversial decision – to open Germany's borders to about one million refugees in 2015, which at the time appeared to threaten her political survival – had the benefit of being admirable from a humanitarian perspective. Compared to more mercurial leaders of other democracies and a growing cast of assertive autocrats throughout the world, Merkel has appeared as a competent, steady and reliable presence. In 2015, she was dubbed 'Chancellor of the Free World' and 'the indispensable European'. In 2020, Germany was, according to some observers, 'doomed to lead' the European Union.[1] Germany's economic and demographic preponderance essentially grants Berlin a veto power over the EU's political direction.

Yet in terms of its security policy, Germany is in a bad way. Years of neglect and structural underfunding have hollowed out the armed forces and created a readiness crisis that will take years to fix. While defence spending has recently increased, those extra funds will be insufficient to meet the requirements identified by defence planners, and the procurement and acquisition process underperforms. Germany is implementing NATO guidelines on defence spending slowly, and occasionally displays a cavalier attitude when it comes to the credibility of NATO's conventional and nuclear deterrence, seemingly impervious to how German national debates resonate among allies. Close partners such as France and the United Kingdom have warned that Germany's restrictive position on arms exports undermines the potential for defence collaboration in Europe, one of Germany's explicit goals.

More fundamentally, Germany's security policy no longer fits the strategic challenges that it now faces. The rise or resurgence of revisionist, repressive and authoritarian powers in China and Russia threatens the Western, United States-led international order upon which Germany's post-war security and prosperity were founded. Many old assumptions about Germany's security and its role in Europe and the wider world no longer apply, but much of the political leadership in Berlin has not yet adjusted to this new reality or appreciated the urgency with which it needs to do so.

Under Vladimir Putin, Russia has re-emerged as a force seeking to undermine NATO and the EU, and with the capability to pose a credible threat to European security and liberal-democratic values. Over the past decade, its armed forces have demonstrated in Syria and Ukraine their ability to learn lessons from earlier conflicts and, following a significant programme of military modernisation, they now present a formidable security challenge to NATO's European members. Moreover, the likely security challenge that Putin's forces pose is not identical to that of the Red Army during the Cold War, meaning that Germany could not simply revive old methods with which to address it.

For many decades, Germany's allies complained about Bonn's (and later Berlin's) overreliance on US forces for its own defence, charging that in security terms it was essentially a free rider. This criticism was both accurate and, in a certain sense, unfair. Following the Second World War, Washington prioritised the economic reconstruction of Europe with German economic power at its heart. This required Germany's neighbours to remain confident that a rebuilt Germany could never again threaten their security. A sizeable presence of American, British and French troops on West German soil therefore served to reassure other Europeans and underpin the continent's recovery. Moreover, in more cynical terms, Germans were correct to assume that, however much US politicians might gripe about Washington's heavy subsidy of Germany's defence, the US would continue to be a reliable guarantor of German and European security, if only out of self-interest and because it had the capability to do so.

This assumption is not as safe as it once seemed. Firstly, Donald Trump's administration (2017–21) demonstrated that a US president could espouse frankly hostile sentiments towards nominal European allies, and even hint at a US withdrawal from NATO. Secondly, and more seriously, a new structural factor that transcends the oscillations of US domestic politics poses a grave challenge to Washington's underwriting of European defence: the rise of China.

China's dramatic economic growth, political aspirations and military ambitions present a long-term threat to German interests through their challenge to the Western order. Under President Xi Jinping, China aims to become a global leader in important high-technology manufacturing and an innovation powerhouse, while also attempting to set global operating standards. Standard-setting, manufacturing and innovation would give Beijing control over considerable elements of economic exchange. They also relate to another of Xi's ambitions; namely, to make China's armed forces capable of fighting and winning wars – displacing the US as the prime security actor in the Indo-Pacific region in the process, leapfrogging the US and its allies in defence-technological terms, and advancing Chinese interests worldwide.

This challenge to Western interests will initially be most visible and consequential in the Indo-Pacific but will inevitably affect the wider world. The Western order, and the values it embodies, is founded upon Western power. As relative Western power declines, it is inevitable that this order will experience more sustained and possibly successful attack. While it would be bold to predict that a risen China would seek to remake the world in its own authoritarian image, it would be even more rash to assume that the Chinese Communist Party (CCP), which considers the democratic ideal a mortal threat, would be indifferent to the relative success of democratic and non-democratic systems even outside its immediate proximity. More broadly, if China were able to sustain its rise and overtake the US in economic and military terms, its increased prestige and clout might have a corrosive effect on the underlying narrative and self-belief of Western liberal democracies.

Germany has benefited, and continues to benefit, from the existence of a US-led Western order that has (for the most part) promoted the open and peaceful exchange of goods and ideas. The German economy is particularly dependent on the safe passage worldwide of its exported goods, whose production is itself dependent on easy access to raw materials. The Western order has nurtured and protected German wealth, liberty and security, and has been a significant factor in Germany's ability to play a meaningful role on the world stage.[2] Any disruption to that order will necessarily pose a threat to German interests, especially when that disruption is led by an authoritarian regime for whom German political, legal and civil values are anathema.

China's rise also poses an indirect but more immediate security challenge to Berlin because of a basic but unavoidable fact: Washington cannot simultaneously contend with a modern, large and capable Chinese military adversary in Asia and continue bearing most of the burden of defending Europe. This shift in US strategic priorities was presaged by Barack Obama's administration's 'pivot' or 'rebalancing' towards Asia, which caused considerable unease in European capitals. The continued growth of China's armed forces will make this strategic dilemma more acute and Washington's guarantee of European security less credible. At present, NATO's European members would struggle to defend their eastern flank in the scenario of a limited conventional war with Russia without drawing upon US capabilities. Replacing those capabilities would incur significant costs and would take somewhere between ten and 20 years. In the scenario of a military confrontation between the US and China, especially one that led to an outright conflict, Europe would be vulnerable to Russian attempts at a land grab, for example in the Baltics, which, were it not promptly reversed, could prompt the disintegration of NATO. More generally, in the context of a US strategically pinned down in the Indo-Pacific, a revanchist Russia would be better placed to use its local conventional (and broader nuclear) superiority to coerce its European neighbours, undermine their independence, and threaten NATO's and the EU's integrity. Given the brute fact of China's rise as a military rival to the US, Europe will need to be able to defend itself. Owing to its size, location and economic power, Germany should naturally play an indispensable role in such efforts. At present, however, it is a largely absent and ineffective actor in efforts to make European self-defence capable and credible. This posture, if sustained, will ultimately pose a dramatic threat to Germany's security.

Thus far, there are few indications that many of Germany's leaders or its populace in general appreciate the seismic nature of the shift in European defence realities triggered by China's rise, or Germany's urgent need to adapt to a fast-approaching new reality. In fact, German discourse is sometimes marked by a worrying degree of ambivalence between the US and its illiberal, undemocratic adversaries. Some espouse a mistaken belief that Germany (and its European allies) can somehow chart a prosperous and quiet middle course between rival superpowers. In the second Merkel cabinet, then-foreign minister Guido Westerwelle (Free Democratic Party–FDP) suggested equidistance or, more prosaically, a pick-and-mix approach to partnerships depending on the issue at hand, as a suitable foreign-policy position for Germany.[3] Academics, including Xuewu Gu at the University of Bonn, promote equidistance as a desirable posture for Germany and Europe as a whole.[4] In January 2021, endorsing a speech by Xi, Merkel argued that:

> I would very much wish to avoid the building of blocs … I don't think it would do justice to many societies if we were to say this is the United States and over there is China and we are grouping around either the one or the other. This is not my understanding of how things ought to be.[5]

The word 'bloc' is, of course, a loaded term intended to evoke the Cold War, but Merkel was essentially arguing that she did not want to choose sides because to do so would be to negate the principle of multilateralism. Of course, when Xi speaks of multilateralism he implies a system designed to ensure 'that international interactions be conducted in accordance with China's perspectives',[6] with a particular emphasis on the principles of non-interference in internal affairs and accepting the uniqueness of each country's system. That is not what Merkel has in mind but, as Constanze Stelzenmüller has noted, Germany 'struggles to reconcile its deeply ingrained instinct to seek equally good relations with friends and foes alike'. Stelzenmüller has argued that Germany's desire to maintain a balance between Europe and the US on the one hand and China and Russia on the other 'undercuts European unity and transatlantic cohesion, alienating Germany's partners and allies … Germany's leaders know this, yet proceed anyway.'[7]

The German government sends conflicting signals about how best to deal with Russia. On the one hand it led efforts to unite Europe in imposing sanctions following Russia's illegal annexation of Crimea in 2014; on the other it insisted that Russia remain a 'partner', while Merkel confidants such as Federal Minister for Economic Affairs and Energy Peter Altmaier publicly questioned the usefulness of such sanctions, alongside an apparent determination to complete projects such as the Nord Stream 2 pipeline despite the strong objection of Berlin's allies.[8] While Germany has joined the club of European countries that have drafted an Indo-Pacific strategy, this almost entirely omits any discussion of military issues.[9]

Germany is trying not to position itself against China while also signalling some concerns about Chinese assertiveness. A German frigate is scheduled to sail through the South China Sea in late 2021 but without crossing into any of the 12-nautical-mile zones around any of the features claimed by China.[10] In 2019, the European Commission described China as simultaneously a cooperation partner, a negotiating partner on certain issues, an economic competitor and a systemic rival.[11] However, so far the desire for commercial advantage has often seemed to take precedence over the defence of political principle, both in Berlin and in Brussels.

With some notable exceptions, on a societal level a notable proportion of Germany's current discourse about security policy, especially in the public domain, remains characterised by a fundamental unseriousness, however well meaning it may sometimes be. It is frequently founded on the assumption, implicit or explicit, that Germany does not need to be capable of defending itself or its nearby allies. It downplays the threats to Germany posed by illiberal, authoritarian states such as China and Russia. It denigrates the role of US military power. In its least edifying manifestations, perhaps marked less by naivety than cynicism, it reveals a desire to enjoy the benefits of a Western world order underpinned by US military power without contributing in a meaningful way to the defence of that order. Running through all of this is the notion that military force and power politics are somehow anachronistic residues of an old world that no longer exists, or at least one from which, since 1945, Germany has wisely chosen to withdraw. While the motivations for these various beliefs vary dramatically in their origin and degree of good faith, the beliefs themselves remain delusional and dangerous, and the task of confronting them facing responsible German leaders is long overdue.

Some senior voices within leadership circles have articulated a desire to address German strategic inertia and an awareness that Germany may need to think harder about what it will take to preserve its own security. In 2020, Minister of Defence Annegret Kramp Karrenbauer pointedly reminded the Munich Security Conference's German audience that, while then-foreign minister Frank-Walter Steinmeier had announced at the same forum in 2014 that Germany 'must be ready for earlier, more decisive and more substantive engagement in the foreign and security policy sphere',[12] Berlin had never acted on this aspiration. She therefore proposed that from 'the Munich "consensus of words" must come "a consensus of action"'.[13]

Wolfgang Schäuble, a veteran German politician and the president of the Bundestag, has remarked that Germany is not a 'dream island' that can afford indifference about the preconditions of its 'liberty and prosperity'.[14]

While such statements resonate with the fairly small strategic community in Berlin outside government and find occasional support in parts of the ministerial bureaucracy, they have not substantively affected Merkel's approach to security matters. Merkel herself has not formulated a conceptually integrated response to Germany's security challenges, nor has she provided authoritative guidance on the strategic purpose of Germany's power. By deploying the Bundeswehr on no fewer than 14 military crisis-management missions abroad, her governing coalition has been able to reassure itself that Germany has indeed shouldered more of the global security burden than it did before. These missions are important, but they do not address the direct security challenges on Germany's horizon. Despite Merkel's many achievements in various spheres over her 16-year leadership, when it comes to elaborating a security policy underpinned by a coherent strategic vision, it appears that she has made little progress.

Several structural factors, pre-dating Merkel's time in office, have contributed to this deficit in strategic thought. The federal republic's institutional organisation provides little dedicated space, in the sense of a specific government forum, to strategy-making and, by dividing responsibility across ministries and the chancellery without creating strong coordinating mechanisms, allows for competing claims on security policy. Germany's historic experience of militarism and destructive excess has created deeply embedded societal preferences that have so far limited the policy choices deemed acceptable by political leaders and the public. German discourse in academia and the think-tank community is heavily influenced by traditions of peace research, international law and regime theory, but provides almost no voice for what is elsewhere recognised as strategic studies. Taken together, such factors create entrenched positions that may often feel morally satisfying to their proponents but are unlikely to engender the agility and impetus for decisive action that Germany now requires.

This book seeks to demonstrate why Germany's leaders should adopt and advocate what we describe as a 'strategic mindset' without further delay. By strategic mindset, we mean an awareness that international affairs are still characterised by power politics and genuine clashes of national interests, not simply misunderstandings; that states are ultimately responsible for their own defence; and that military power is a legitimate component of statecraft, whether employed (primarily) as a credible deterrent or (occasionally and to the minimum degree possible) as an instrument of force used in order to safeguard national interests and the interests of other like-minded, liberal-democratic states.

Germany does already possess a 'strategic culture': the ideas and preferences regarding the use of armed force shared by a society, which influence what is regarded as acceptable foreign-policy behaviour.[15] Unfortunately, that culture is insufficiently strategic in nature. While Germany will never share an identical strategic culture to those of other leading Western nations, it should seek to foster one that is at least compatible with them, and which can allow Germans to perceive international affairs through a strategic lens. Moreover, Germany cannot afford to make this transition at a gentle, evolutionary pace. The threat to its security posed by an assertive Russia and China's rise is more imminent than often imagined, and it will take time to ensure that Berlin (and its European allies) are adequately prepared to handle it. Germany therefore requires a rapid paradigm shift in its strategic thought, or a contemporary version of what Quentin Skinner has described as the 'Machiavellian revolution'.[16]

Niccolò Machiavelli is best known for his advice that Italian Renaissance leaders should abandon the classical notion of *virtus* (essentially featuring moderation and justice as the key characteristics guiding government action) in favour of the context-dependent concept of *virtù*, which, for Machiavelli's readers, entailed the practice of amoral power politics. Yet perhaps the most relevant part of his legacy is that he offered a fresh conceptual vocabulary, arguing that contemporary leaders needed to relinquish their outdated and dangerously self-restraining methods when defending their interests and values against those who, by default, ignored such otherwise admirable approaches. Put differently, he designed his *virtù* to equip leaders with techniques to survive a dangerous period of political transition.[17] While some elements of Germany's self-conception as a 'civilian power' (*Zivilmacht*) – as analyst Hanns W. Maull has termed it – may continue to provide useful intellectual underpinnings for the country's broader practice of international affairs, Berlin may need something along the lines of Machiavelli's intellectual revolution to deal with the challenges it faces, and it now has an opportunity to revise its outdated approach to security policy.

We are *not* arguing that Germany should adopt an amoral, cynical or militaristic foreign and security policy. Rather, we believe that Berlin should acknowledge that other powerful states do act in this way; that these states seek to challenge liberal values and the Western order; and that, to defend liberal ends, realistic means ultimately supported by credible military power are both justified and necessary. Germany's power should be allied with moral purpose. While it is admirable that Merkel has called on Germany to take on 'more responsibility',[18] when it comes to security questions, incremental or misdirected increases to defence spending will be insufficient if there is no clear vision of what the armed forces are for. As Germany's pursuit of more responsibility has so far lacked a real vision or purpose, its strategic trajectory has largely been aimless. Western predominance – based on economic, techno-logical and military superiority – which serves the purpose of safeguarding individual freedom and democracy as its non-negotiable core values, should be the essence of such a vision. Germany's historic national responsibility should not be interpreted as the dogmatic rejection of all military force (going beyond a rejection of the pernicious doctrine of mili-tarism), rather it should be understood as the defence of the Western liberal values that Germany once sought to destroy and of the Western order, based on those values, that rebuilt and welcomed Germany as an essential and valued member, and which is now once again under threat. The defence of that order, which has nurtured German liberty and prosper-ity, would represent not just a defence of German values but a defence of German interests. Germany's contribution should be to wed its commitment to liberal values to an understanding of the role of power, including military power.

Many might argue – correctly – that Germany's contribution to the defence (and positive future evolution) of the Western order could and should take many forms, most of them non-military. Germany can indeed make a difference in many ways, including but not limited to geo-economic statecraft, applying its diplomatic weight to coalition-building, and leading the way in the establishment of technical standards or the reform of international law so that it remains relevant to contempo-rary challenges. Moreover, any German 'grand strategy' that seeks to maintain Western leadership and ensure the survival of Western values in the coming decades will need to address broader challenges to Germany's economic or social model, upon whose strength its military and diplomatic power necessarily rests. These challenges might include, for example, how the German economy will adapt to the replacement of the internal combustion engine over the next two decades. Nevertheless, rather than seek to encompass in a necessarily telegraphic style the totality of an overarching German foreign and security strategy, this book focuses on the question of security policy. In part, this is because this question will encounter the most intellectual resistance within Germany while simultaneously being one of the most urgent and unavoidable challenges facing it today. It is in this realm that the gap between Germany's potential and its performance is greatest. While Germany is good at many things and should exploit its competitive advantages in any way possible to advance the common interests of Berlin and its Western allies, it can no longer afford to outsource defence and security challenges to others. Germany can and should do many things to help defend the Western order and contribute to its future positive development, but an indispensable element of that effort will be ensuring that Europe can defend itself militarily – and Europe cannot do so without Germany.

It is important to remember, of course, that while the administration of US President Joe Biden provides an opportunity to renew the transatlantic partnership and imbue it with an invigorated sense of shared purpose – a common endeavour to protect liberal values against their enemies – this revived alliance should not be understood as the instigator of a new cold war in which Russia and China are to be opposed categorically in all spheres.[19] Some shared transnational threats, most obviously climate change and infectious disease, will require cooperation, rather than competition or confrontation, between the great powers. Western publics will be more ready to support their leadership in long-standing confrontations with authoritarian powers over non-negotiable principles of liberal democracy if they realise that their leaders are also willing to work with those powers for a shared common good that cannot be obtained independently. That said, European cooperation with major powers is likely to be more mutually fruitful if those powers are aware that Europe is doing so from a position of military strength and security, not one of weakness and supplication.

Critics may object that neither the German public nor its leadership are remotely interested in – much less ready for – a more strategic understanding of the world. This would be to overlook the reality that, in recent years, there have been voices at senior levels whose perception differs significantly from the dominant narrative.[20] Moreover, while Winston Churchill's supposed remark that 'the difference between mere management and true leadership is communication' is probably apocryphal, the sentiment is accurate: future German leaders must communicate to their people that their interests and the Western order of which they are a vital member are ultimately at stake. If they do so successfully, then it is not entirely unrealistic to believe that looming worries may turn into popular support for new policies.

In what follows, we examine why many Germans understand their role in the world in the way that they do, and suggest other, possibly more constructive framings of German history and responsibilities; examine the causes and consequences of current shortfalls and failures in German defence spending and procurement; propose a more strategic understanding of threats from China and Russia; and suggest realistic ways by which Germany could make an essential contribution to Europe's ability to defend itself, including by participating in more imaginative and effective means of nuclear deterrence.

We recognise that many of our compatriots (as well as observers in Germany's partner states) will disagree with our arguments. We welcome such disagreement and all good-faith efforts to engage with the ideas discussed here. Germans have both an opportunity and an obligation to ask, and answer, a simple question: with the return of great-power competition and possibly conflict, and a weakened commitment to and occasional blatant disregard for the rules-based order even by some of those states who originally constructed it, what is German power for?[21] As Chancellor Merkel's time in office comes to a close, Germany's new political leadership should initiate a serious, realistic and mature debate among the German people about their country's place in and responsibilities towards the world, the emerging threats to the security and prosperity that they now take for granted, and how Germany should best address these threats in the forthcoming era whose outline is now taking shape. There is no more time to waste.

CHAPTER ONE

The sources of German conduct

It is easy to understand why outsiders often consider Germany an exemplar of modern, mature democratic government. John Kampfner's *Why the Germans Do It Better: Notes from a Grown-Up Country* (2020) is a typical example of such foreign admiration, arguing that Germany's successes derive from a combination of its traditional 'German efficiency' with notions of humility and quiet competence.[1] Kampfner provides compelling evidence that Germany's workers are considerably more productive than their British counterparts, its national wealth more equitably distributed, and its average educational standards significantly higher. While the start of Germany's COVID-19 vaccination programme in 2021 was an unusual example of administrative incompetence, its earlier management of the pandemic helped it to emerge with a significantly lower death rate than in France, the US and especially the UK.

Berlin's foreign admirers have a point: in questions of domestic policy, Germany *does* get many things right, it demonstrates considerable maturity of judgement and its foreign allies could learn much from it. However, when it comes to the ability to confront strategic challenges in the international realm honestly and directly, few foreign observers would agree that the Germans 'do it better'. While many Germans might consider their country's approach to security policy – marked by a reflexive aversion to perceived bellicosity – more advanced than that of their allies, a more accurate description would be 'immature'.

Military force is integral to the exercise of national power and a core aspect of national strategy. While directly relevant only to a limited set of problems, armed force in certain circumstances is part of the solution, often in combination with other levers of state power. This basic reality is well understood in London, Paris and Warsaw, but also in Beijing, Moscow and Washington DC. German security-policy discourse represents an outlier in that the intrinsic link between diplomacy and the use of armed force, which forms one of the foundations of statecraft, is under-developed or even rejected.[2] Back in 1961, Sir Michael Howard, reviewing Helmut Schmidt's book *Verteidigung oder Vergeltung: Ein deutscher Beitrag zum strategischen Problem der NATO* for the IISS journal *Survival*, suggested that 'a renaissance of German strategic studies is overdue'.[3] Sadly for Germany, his hope has not yet been fulfilled.

Germany's strategic culture is sometimes depicted as underdeveloped or even non-existent.[4] This view is unhelpful because it underestimates the problem. If Germany had no strategic culture, the ideational vacuum could be filled with relative ease. However, it does have a predominant strategic culture: one that generates preferences for government behaviour that are ill-suited to the requirements of modern security and defence policy. This means that replacing or adjusting it will be harder than simply filling a gap.

Writing in 2020, Ellis S. Krauss and Hanns W. Maull suggested that Germany's strategic-preference set can be summarised as 'never again', meaning the rejection of military expansionism and totalitarianism; 'never alone', meaning any action must be embedded in multilateral structures; and 'politics before force'.[5] While these precepts sound admirable in theory, in practice the result has been that the dominant narrative of German security policy is that there are no military solutions to conflicts and crises.[6] Whenever this dogma clashes with reality, the German security-policy debate adjusts somewhat, allowing for parliamentary mandates for the deployment of Bundeswehr personnel or military assistance to beleaguered partners. Reactive muddling through when previous choices no longer work might be acceptable when threats are non-existent. But this approach is not enough when Germany faces fundamental threats to its security.

One reason why the strategic debate has remained largely sterile is that too many Germans subscribe to an inaccurate and unhelpful understanding of the lessons of their country's history. For example, too often a laudable rejection of militarism shades into an implicit or explicit pacifism that presents itself as a responsible and moral alternative to the use of military force more broadly. As a prominent German commentator suggested in late 2020, pacifism is the 'cudgel' used to suppress a more nuanced and more substantial debate, offering in strategic terms a decidedly unhelpful dichotomy between good (peace) and bad (war).[7]

To understand why many Germans have found it difficult to conceive of foreign and security policy in strategic terms (or, as we would put it, to adopt a strategic mindset), it is useful to examine the powerful historical factors inhibiting them from doing so, and to consider possible constructive reframings of the contemporary implications of Germany's historical legacy that would better equip it to address the strategic challenges it faces. It is also important to consider political, institutional, constitutional and educational structural factors that have reinforced Germany's strategic culture and will complicate any effort to adapt it.

The 'lessons' of history

In a 1981 lecture on 'the lessons of history', Howard observed that 'all we believe about the present depends on what we believe about the past'.[8] This insight is deceptively simple but has profound implications. While we argue that Germany must adopt a strategic mindset that accepts the legitimacy of military force as an instrument of statecraft, it is vital to acknowledge the historical realities that explain why many Germans remain understandably wary of doing so.

Germany emerged as a unitary state following three victorious Prussian-led wars against Denmark, Austria and France in the 1860s and 1870s. The new German Empire dominated the European continent not only economically and militarily but also in matters of culture, science and technology. Despite these achievements, many Germans yearned for their state to become a global, imperial power (*Weltmacht*), and the decades before 1914 were marked by increasing tensions with the existing global hegemon, the British Empire, as well as a converse German anxiety that a rising land power to their east, the Russian Empire, would soon eclipse and ultimately subjugate them. Less than 60 years after its founding in a series of wars, the German Empire was broken and humiliated by its defeat in another, much more destructive conflict.[9] A century later, the origins of the First World War are still fiercely debated. While most contemporary historians would reject the charge (levelled by the war's victors and codified in the Treaty of Versailles) that Germany was solely to blame, the opposing claim of systemic or universal responsibility, often combined with the argument that European leaders unwittingly 'sleepwalked' into the conflict, is also unconvincing – although a revived version of this thesis has recently enjoyed significant popular success in Germany, including with Chancellor Merkel herself.[10]

While rivers of historians' ink will continue to be shed on which European state bore most culpability for the First World War, it has never been plausibly argued that any other than Germany was primarily responsible for the Second World War, a cataclysm of unparalleled destruction that left Europe in ruins and tens of millions dead. Moreover, during this war Germany combined the mechanised mass murder of civilians on an industrial scale with countless individual acts of unspeakable sadism perpetrated by a significant proportion of its armed and police forces. Contrary to later myths indulged in by some Germans and foreigners, these atrocities were not restricted to Nazi zealots in SS units but were often conducted by regular German soldiers.[11] German militarism destroyed Germany itself, brutalised Europe, and ensured that the continent would remain under the sway of rival superpowers – the US and the Soviet Union – for another half-century.

The war's supposed lessons differed for each of its participant states. It seemed reasonable for Britons or Americans, for example, to infer that the use of military force against unappeasable authoritarians was not just legitimate but essential; while for most Germans it seemed irrefutable that the pursuit of geopolitical power and the glorification of military strength had led to their country's nemesis and almost extinguished Western civilisation in Europe. It is therefore unsurprising that West Germans, as well as their occupiers, determined that German militarism and the desire to dominate Europe (and eventually the world) must never be allowed to emerge again.

The intellectual and emotional impact of the notion of a 'collective guilt' for Nazi acts and the desire to atone for these misdeeds (perhaps held more sincerely by later generations of Germans) was reinforced by the blunt political reality of Germany's occupation and partition by the victorious powers. Although West Germany was recognised as a sovereign state in 1949 and later became a core member of NATO – and its economic recovery was considered a key part of Western Europe's resistance to the looming Soviet threat – the Allied determination to suppress any persistent, latent German urges for dominance and to reassure other European states was expressed in Lord Ismay's famous remark that NATO was created to 'keep the Soviet Union out, the Americans in, and the Germans down'.[12] Moreover, while the new Bundesrepublik was expected to play a major role in any future war against the Soviets and their allies, the Bundeswehr was designed to mount a defence of its own territory against a Warsaw Pact invasion – not to participate in offensive foreign campaigns. For the Bundeswehr to play its part in NATO, it did not have to project military power abroad – Germany would have been the battlefield, had the Cold War turned hot. While West Germany was a key member of the US-led Western order, and benefited greatly from it, in terms of statecraft it was acceptable for Germany to be what Maull later termed a 'civilian power' (*Zivilmacht*). During the Cold War, 'dependence and subordination … became the hallmark of German foreign and military policy', a welcome contrast to the 'would-be hegemonist in Europe' of the past.[13]

This civilian self-image survived the end of the Cold War and German reunification. In 1991, the IISS *Strategic Survey* asked: 'Now that Germany, its nationhood restored, has regained its unity and full sovereignty, what are the Germans going to do with it?'[14] The immediate answer was that the future would be like the recent past, only more so – contemporary decision-makers in Germany and most of its partners judged that continuity was of primary importance, not least to make the increased weight of a united Germany in Europe palatable to others. The end of the Cold War might not have looked like the end of history, but it did look like a liberation, and one that would, in the contemporaneous words of Josef Joffe, 'enhance the peculiar sources of German strength. The political value of economic potency and geographic position is bound to soar as the previously dominant assets of power – the *ultima ratio* of military force – are scaled down or withdrawn from Europe.'[15] The sentiment at the time was that Germany had achieved its core objectives – it was now unified and secure because it was surrounded by European partners and allies. The world at the time looked less threatening, the utility of armed force reduced and the major upheaval in international relations like a security gain for Germany. The experience of negotiating unification further strengthened the view that ever deeper and stronger multilateral ties would provide Germany with more, not less, room for manoeuvre in foreign-policy terms.[16] Peaceful reunification had required Soviet acquiescence and goodwill. From the perspective of reunited Germans, it was reasonable to assume that Moscow's trust in West German intentions had been strengthened by Bonn's earlier efforts to cooperate with adversaries (such as Willy Brandt's Ostpolitik) as well as repeated and sincere gestures of atonement and reparation for earlier German aggression.

While the discourse concerning armed force in German security policy has shifted somewhat since 1991 (as discussed further in the next chapter), some (such as Krauss and Maull) suggest that the *Zivilmacht* concept has continued to serve Germany well and weathered significant change in Germany's international-security environment since the end of the Cold War.[17] Those Germans who condemned outright the use of military force doubtless drew some vindication from the outcome of the US-led wars of the first two decades of the twenty-first century. While these wars were launched with the stated goal of defeating terrorism or replacing dictatorship with democracy, in practice they were largely strategic failures that did not achieve their stated objectives, failed to advance US or Western interests, resulted in significant numbers of civilian deaths, and featured instances of mistreatment, torture and murder of detainees.[18]

It is important to recognise the benefits of the societal and political preferences that enabled Germany's rehabilitation among civilised nations after the Second World War, supported its economic regeneration and made its peaceful reunification more likely. Yet it is also important to recognise that these preferences, and the strategic culture they represent, no longer provide a successful foundation for the strategic choices the country now faces and is likely to face in the future. In particular, the notion that Germany can or should embrace a de facto pacifism, in which the use of force is considered inherently immoral, is a self-indulgence that must persist no longer.

While there are obvious practical reasons why this is so, pacifism is also not just an impractical but a deeply irresponsible position. It rests on the assumption either that there are no external aggressors both willing and able to subjugate others with armed force; that it is better to submit to than to resist attempts to subvert or remove one's hard-earned rights and freedoms; or that another actor can be relied upon to shoulder the burden of defending those rights while one continues to enjoy the illusion of moral purity. Implicitly or explicitly subscribing to such a doctrine was morally problematic in Germany's recent past, but this could be sustained because there were few obvious hard security threats to German and European security and because other actors, most notably the US, *were* willing and able to shoulder that burden. Given the changing realities in global politics, pacifism is now not just an immoral doctrine, but a dangerous and unsustainable one.

Other misapplications of history and conceptual confusions complicate contemporary German statecraft. Public opinion remains deeply divided with regards to Russia, for example.

Roughly equal shares of the population feel threatened by Russia, somewhat threatened, or not threatened at all. A relative majority is against limiting the trade and economic relationship with Russia but a relative majority of citizens is also against lending more support to Russia's positions.[19] This split in public opinion, with views ranging from fear to great warmth, also affects elites in policy, business and culture.[20] A pragmatic willingness to engage in diplomacy and explore the possibility of cooperating over shared interests with states such as Russia should not be conflated with a misplaced self-conception as a 'bridge' between a liberal-democratic ally that helped West Germany to rejoin the community of free and prosperous nations and an autocracy that installed a police state in East Germany, even if one's ancestors did inflict terrible crimes against that autocracy's citizens three-quarters of a century ago.[21] At some point, considering oneself a perpetrator and another a victim for eternity, no matter how that supposed victim now behaves or if it threatens one's own security, crosses over from understandable remorse into self-indulgent masochism.

History has assigned Germans many responsibilities. They have a responsibility to accept national liability for the consequences of earlier German militarism and aggression, to abjure any repetition of such behaviour and to make reparation to the victims of such behaviour. Germany has so far succeeded in fulfilling this responsibility – and it should continue to do so. We are not suggesting that Germans should now consider the past a closed book or their responsibilities for past actions discharged. Germany's atonement for past misdeeds and determination to educate fresh generations about previous traumas has been exemplary and should not be reversed. But the responsibility to heed the lessons of the past does not absolve Germans from their responsibilities to the present and future. Several generations after the end of the Second World

War, and with new threats on the horizon, it is reasonable to venture that an additional, complementary understanding of national responsibility is appropriate and constructive.

This understanding is 'the responsibility to defend': the obligation to defend the liberal values that prevailed against earlier German onslaughts, and to defend the Western order, based on those values, which rebuilt Germany from the ashes and of which Germany has been an integral member for decades.[22] Germans have a responsibility not only to refrain from militarism and aggression, but also to remember that unappeasable dictators do exist and that such leaders can use rational means to pursue what liberals would consider irrational ends, and to help their allies prevent further such dictatorships from threatening liberalism's future. Germany has a special role to play. That role is not to fantasise that it can exist indefinitely as a historical anomaly – a pacifist great power free to ignore the role of armed force in statecraft. The conditions that could allow such a mindset were only temporary – an aberration enabled by the unusual role of the US in German and European security since 1945. Instead, this more sustainable, special role would be as a responsible, liberal state that combines strategic heft with moral purpose.

The strategic mindset we believe Germany must adopt would be an indispensable tool that would allow it to fulfil this role. We do not, however, underestimate the significant political and structural challenges in doing so.

Structural factors

Significant political, constitutional, educational and institutional factors will make the development of an evolved German strategic culture more difficult, although not impossible. In the political realm, much can depend on the personal worldview and political priorities of a current chancellor. German chancellors can remain in office for long periods compared to most of their Western counterparts. Konrad Adenauer (1949–63) and Helmut Kohl (1982–98) were the most obvious examples of this phenomenon before Merkel, who will have been in power for 16 years when she stands down. These long terms allow for a chancellor's worldview to impress itself on government.

Some might argue that Merkel's worldview may have inhibited the development of a new strategic mindset. When Russia annexed Crimea in 2014, Merkel interpreted these events as a tragic aberration of historic trends – a throwback to the nineteenth and twentieth centuries when conflicts over spheres of influence and territory were common, a condition that had since 'been overcome'. In the twenty-first century, Merkel argued, 'lived globalisation' (*gelebte Globalisierung*) implied that states, explicitly including Russia, must tackle big challenges together and benefit more from cooperation than from going it alone. A state acting against this logic of harmony would ultimately, Merkel argued three times in one speech, 'hurt itself'.[23] Merkel has referred to Russia as a 'partner' throughout her tenure, including after the invasion of Crimea and the attempted murder of Russian dissident Alexei Navalny in 2020. Her defenders might counter that her exhortations for Russia to see the error of its ways represented less naivety than a diplomatic strategy to isolate and condemn it when military measures against it were neither feasible nor desirable; and that, since 2014, Germany has played a leading role in European diplomatic efforts to support Ukraine.[24]

Moreover, some observers of German politics argue that, while Merkel has extraordinary powers to guide the country's politico-strategic direction (under article 65 of the Grundgesetz, the constitution of the Bundesrepublik), in reality that same article also seriously constrains her freedom of leadership. Its second sentence, which establishes the *Ressortprinzip*, referring policy-related matters exclusively to the cabinet member running the respective ministry, has seriously undermined the chancellor's power. Some would argue that Germany's eight-year coalition-based government (with the Social Democratic Party–SPD), which was bound by a treaty outlining the coalition's main tenets, have made it impossible for Merkel to provide and execute straightforward guidance on Berlin's strategy-related direction, given the SPD's increasing reluctance to recognise military force as a legitimate instrument of statecraft.[25] Despite a German chancellor's formal powers, even a weaker political partner can impose its will by threatening to dissolve the coalition. As the chancellor has no legal powers to execute direction over a particular ministry, only political ones, they are to a great extent dependent on consensual decision-making.[26] Should the September 2021 general election generate a governing coalition that is more closely aligned on security- and defence-policy priorities than the Christian Democratic Union and Christian Social Union (CDU/CSU) and SPD were before it, the coordination challenge in this realm could become more manageable. Reinforcing the lack of political consensus within many German governments is a lack of institutional focus: national-security policy remains largely uncoordinated across the various relevant ministries and suffers from the absence of a dedicated government forum.

It is sometimes argued that public opinion presents a strong obstacle to more far-reaching changes in Germany's strategic choices, as it constrains the practical options open to its politicians. As recently as 2020, some scholars argued that emerging discussions on a more active security-policy role were largely an elite discourse disconnected from the preferences of the wider public who did not support a greater degree of activism.[27] While it is certainly true that democratic governments need a sustainable level of majority public support to govern successfully, it is not clear why political leaders should follow, rather than lead, public opinion. But more importantly, while accepting that public opinion will sometimes be a constraint and sometimes an enabler of political action, the data no longer actually supports the notion that public opinion is in fact an obstacle. Across various opinion polls conducted in recent years, a permissive consensus has emerged, especially among the younger generation, that would support a more active German foreign and security policy, including a stronger role in international conflict resolution.[28] Regardless of who occupies the chancellery in Berlin, consistent and sustained communication to engage members of the public in a conversation about the international challenges to their security and, more widely, the current state of the world, remains a deficit that should be addressed.

Beyond political and constitutional constraints on its leaders, at present Germany features a relatively uniform academic and institutional environment that has contributed to an excessively narrow range of intellectual alternatives to security shibboleths. This is not a controversial opinion. Indeed, in his 2014 speech to the Munich Security Conference, best known for sounding the alarm that Germany needed to assume 'more responsibility', then-president Joachim Gauck argued that 'to find its proper course in these difficult times', Germany needed 'above all intellectual resources. It needs minds, institutions and forums.' He explicitly targeted German universities, averse as they have been to matters related to strategy and security, and asked: 'I wonder if it isn't time for all the universities to mobilise more than a handful of chairs where German foreign policy can be analysed.'[29]

More than seven years after Gauck's remarks, there is still not a single German university department that offers any course that systematically teaches 'strategic studies'. A database search of some 12,500 degree programmes at full universities in

Germany conducted in early 2021 shows only one war-studies degree programme (at the University of Potsdam) and two more programmes that are explicit security-studies degrees, both of them at the Bundeswehr University Munich. There are also nine degree programmes that fall into the peace-research tradition.[30] Indeed, it is notable that two visiting professorships in strategic studies funded by the German Academic Exchange Service (DAAD), a non-profit institution supporting German academics conducting research abroad (and non-German academic visitors coming to Germany), are located in the US and Israel. Germany does therefore support German professors of strategic studies, but primarily outside Germany itself, in countries with strong traditions in that discipline.[31] The Henry Kissinger Professorship for Security and Strategic Studies at the University of Bonn, funded by a grant from the federal foreign office and the federal ministry of defence, and the associated Center for Advanced Security, Strategic and Integration Studies, which also has a connection to the DAAD position in Israel, could be a promising development. Another notable exception is the Institute for Security Policy at Kiel University, which has been a hub for several recent security-policy-focused PhD theses, and whose director also edits the primary German-language strategic-analysis journal, *SIRIUS*.

The research of many of the most influential German international-relations scholars is based on the concept of global governance.[32] It tends to view politics through the prism of global problems and of states' supposedly shared interests and goals. When viewed through this lens, the study of international affairs is essentially understood to entail rational problem-solving related to transnational issues such as climate, health or trade. This rests on various underlying assumptions, including that there is a shared global agenda, and that since much of international politics is the rational and technocratic management of issues through international institutions, international leadership by any one state or group of states becomes less significant. In a world of global governance, the use of military force is considered at best redundant and at worst archaic and destructive and is, therefore, almost completely absent from such analyses. This, broadly speaking, has been the predominant approach taught at German universities.[33] Such a perspective fails to recognise that international organisations embody decisions by states about particular political arrangements, which in turn are 'encoded into rules' by history.[34] Rather than being ahistorical, eternal realities, contemporary international institutions are dependent on a Western hegemony now under threat.

Funding structures play a significant role in Germany's intellectual landscape as it relates to strategic issues. Unlike in many other Western states, a single large federal agency, the German Research Foundation (DFG), is the main funding entity supporting research on international relations as an academic subject. Its annual budget – €3.3 billion in 2019 – is vast and grants it a commensurate impact on research priorities.[35] It has more than 16 times the size of the budget of the next-largest and private foundation (VW), which funded €200 million in research (including on international affairs) in 2020.[36] With the Fritz Thyssen Foundation's funding at €17.1m, the Robert Bosch Foundation's at €105m and the Gerda Henkel Foundation's at €18.2m in 2019,[37] the DFG's preponderance is overwhelming. The large political parties' foundations are not involved in funding postdoctoral research activities at all, magnifying the DFG's influence even further. Crucially, its ideational impact is linked to the predominant scholarly interests pursued by those senior professors who compose the DFG's selection committees. Their research interests are often driven by the assumptions of global governance described above.

This quasi-monopolistic funding structure has had a profound effect on the discipline of international relations in Germany. It is of course true that a junior postdoctoral scholar in the English-speaking world, seeking a career as an assistant professor, will face many challenges in their efforts to obtain tenure through publications and winning research funding. Their counterpart in Germany, however, faces a different landscape. Their professional goal is a more remote one: a full professorship, with no tenured positions as a refuge of professional security beforehand. These German early-career scholars have even more incentive, therefore, to adhere to the intellectual mainstream because they are largely dependent on global-governance-oriented funding. It is likely that such a scholar will understand their incentive structure to be influenced by the conceptual mindset that attracts the majority of the funding upon which their career depends.

The landscape of policy-oriented think tanks in Berlin is certainly wide and diverse. Nevertheless, the largest ones, including those anchored in the political parties' foundations,[38] have often struggled to provide security-related analysis that advances the analytical discourse or challenges government policy for several reasons. Firstly, in the absence of an accepted culture of private donations for strategy-related research, public funding is their near-exclusive source of revenue. Secondly, the primary task of these think tanks is to advise the government or to inform public discourse in alignment with the agenda of their respective political party. While there are several challenger think tanks – mostly recent additions to the marketplace of ideas, whose practices and business models differ from the traditional German approach – their influence has so far been limited. It is therefore unsurprising that an assessment of foreign- and security-policy think tanks in Germany concluded in September 2020 that there was a conspicuous and long-standing lack of security and strategic-studies research and a perceived unwillingness to criticise government policy.[39]

Ultimately, the constructive, thoughtful and realistic input of German academics and think tanks will be essential if Germany is to enjoy a healthy public debate about vital interests and the use of force. In practical terms, however, any meaningful reform of German security policy first requires a clear-eyed assessment of how and why Germany has underperformed so significantly in this realm in recent years, and the current state of its armed forces. It is impossible to plan for the future without appreciating the condition of Germany's current security policy: one that is perhaps more alarming than is often realised.

CHAPTER TWO

Germany's troubled security policy

The absence of a strategic mindset in Germany has had consequences. Among them are a Bundeswehr with glaring capability gaps, including deep readiness challenges, and an immature public discourse about the use of force in foreign and security policy. While the Bundeswehr is often capable of thinking clearly about strategic challenges and the military capabilities required to meet them, the commensurate political commitment to secure the requisite funding or make difficult decisions on capability shortfalls is usually absent. German security policy has often been driven less by thoughtful consideration of real strategic challenges than by a desire to shape or respond to foreign perceptions of Berlin. Successive German governments, including those led by Angela Merkel, have considered it important to be considered a reliable ally and supporter of multilateral efforts by peers to uphold international peace and stability. The requirements of that role, and of being a responsible member of the Euro-Atlantic community of states, evolve over time, not least because the international security environment and the associated expectations of partners change with it. German leaders in the 1990s and early 2000s certainly felt the pressure to adapt. German participation in international crisis-management operations; attempts to reform the armed forces to be fit for modern operations; debates over defence-spending levels; and discussions about parliamentary oversight of international Bundeswehr deployments reflected this clash of domestic preferences and external adaption pressures.

Doing the minimum required to maintain one's national reputation, however, will no longer suffice. German Minister of Defence Annegret Kramp-Karrenbauer argued in October 2020 that 'we are prepared to change our policies, have tough debates, adapt to new situations, and accept new realities when it comes to defence. But we will not stand for disruptive politics.'[1] While she made these remarks in light of the divisive politics on display in the US on the eve of the 2020 presidential election, her statement is noteworthy because it reveals certain important perceptions about the nature of change. Kramp-Karrenbauer equated disruption with negative change that cannot be controlled and will lead to undesirable outcomes. For her, change is ideally associated with adjustment, the preservation of established positions and continuity. To be fair, many conservative politicians in Germany and other democracies share this outlook. But such incrementalism is an insufficient response to a world that, as Merkel argued at the CDU party conference in 2016, has been knocked 'out of joint', in which 'power centres are realigning' and which 'needs to sort itself out'. At that time, Merkel asked 'what should actually be done now?'[2] While breaking with past practice can be difficult, in Germany the diagnosis by some politicians of revolutionary international change that will produce more instability and threats has not yet led to a commensurate solution: fundamental adjustments to security policy. The perceived wisdom, as expressed by Kramp-Karrenbauer, that the underlying logic of change is continuity, explains why novel threats, technologies and uses of force in Germany tend to be embedded in past narratives, concepts and political choices.[3] Thus, when the pendulum swung back over the course of the last decade, and the processes that had led to multilateralism and the advancing codification of a rules-based international order went into reverse, great-power conflict intensified, and the utility of armed force (or the threat of it) was demonstrated on battlefields in Asia, Europe, the Middle East and North Africa, the challenges for Germany's strategic position were profound.

During the Cold War, the German armed forces were optimised for collective defence within NATO, which, due to Germany's geographical position, was equivalent to territorial defence. If there were a major war, the Bundeswehr would not have needed to project power abroad because the war would have been fought on its home turf. Preparing for this eventuality was in Germany's interest and in the interest of its allies – external expectations and internal preferences were well aligned. The Bundeswehr had to be large but essentially static. In 1990, Germany had more combat battalions in active service (215) than Europe's two most capable military powers combined: France (106) and the United Kingdom (94).[4]

When the focus shifted to force projection for crisis-management purposes during the 1990s and early 2000s, Germany was slow to adapt: the external demand for military power projection did not align with domestic preferences, and the military capabilities that did exist were not well-suited to those new requirements. Ironically, by the time Germany had begun to make conceptual sense of military tasks such as counter-insurgency or counter-terrorism, Russia had annexed Crimea and provided support for armed insurgents in eastern Ukraine. The spectre resurfaced of a conventional Russian military threat to European security that required a conventional military response. As the threat vectors multiply, international developments continue to outpace Germany's debate on the role of the armed forces and the purpose of military power.

Military operations and their purpose

The very essence of military force – the one factor that distinguishes the armed forces from any other instrument of state power – is that in extreme circumstances soldiers are mandated to deliver death and destruction on a large scale. While the notion that the ultimate measure for the Bundeswehr is the ability to prevail in combat is integral to German strategy documents, political leaders are more likely to refer to soldiers as citizens in uniform (*Bürger in Uniform*) than as warriors. Sönke Neitzel, professor of military history at the University of Potsdam, has suggested that the idea that the soldier is a 'global social worker, who as saviour, mediator, and protector helps worldwide', is popular, while the professional identity of soldiers as warriors is de-emphasised.[5] As practitioners and scholars alike have suggested, German public discourse struggles to address military means in general, let alone the application of armed force in any specific context.[6] This has important consequences because it suggests that the purpose of military force is not properly conceptualised as a lever of national power that German politicians must sometimes employ. The *ultima ratio* of applying military force is sometimes misinterpreted as suggesting that armed force should only be used *after* all other means have failed. Many Germans therefore perceive the use of armed force as a course of action that runs counter to the federal republic's civilian-power self-image, and sometimes as a preference foisted upon it by more extrovert German allies, including France, the UK and the US.

That armed force is a necessary complement to other instruments of state power and is required for softer power mechanisms to be effective at all bears repeating in the context of Germany's security-policy debate. Force can be employed to achieve peace, and inaction also represents a choice, with consequences that can bring suffering – but this uncomfortable insight is rarely discussed in Berlin. Germany's historical militarism, and the so-called culture of restraint to which it has contributed, impedes this discussion. However, as Wolfgang Ischinger, one of Germany's most seasoned retired diplomats, has suggested, at some point having had a difficult childhood is no longer good enough as an excuse.[7] German President Frank-Walter Steinmeier recently stressed that those who would like to promote a cooperative international order will need to do so from a position of strength.[8] Steinmeier was speaking about Europe, not Germany as such, and about unity and resolve rather than questions of armed force. In a world of great risk and multiple threats, the refusal to conceive of defence and military matters as a dimension that also requires unity and resolve means that Germany does not contribute what it can and should to efforts to promote the world order it desires. Germany probably represents the greatest unused hard-power potential of European nations, simply because it chooses to punch so far below its weight.

When it comes to the use of force, the questions of when to act, with what means and under what circumstances remain challenging for the German people. In 2005, then German president Horst Köhler suggested that Germans trusted their armed forces but showed at best a 'benign disinterest' (*freundliches Desinteresse*) when it came to their activities.[9] His assessment still holds. Polling data commissioned by the federal government shows that, every year since 2005, some 75–83% of Germans have reported a positive general attitude towards the Bundeswehr. In 2020 (the most recent data year available), however, some 49% of respondents answered that they had never heard of NATO's Enhanced Forward Presence mission, in which Germany is one of the lead nations, and 50% had never heard of NATO's Baltic Air Policing operation, to which Germany has routinely contributed for years.[10] It is notable that since 2015 the share of respondents who said they felt well informed about international Bundeswehr deployments decreased from 40% to 16%.[11] The Bundeswehr has participated in more than 50 international missions since the end of the Cold War, but German citizens do not seem to be particularly aware of or interested in this fact. Interestingly, although since 2015 (a period coinciding with Russian military action in Ukraine and Syria) a majority of Germans (some years a relative majority, occasionally an absolute majority) have supported higher defence spending, public opinion remains split on whether or not Russia represents a security threat to Germany.[12] China only emerged as an item in government polling on security policy in 2019, with 25% of Germans considering that China's foreign and security policy does present a security threat and 35% considering that it does not (with the remaining 40% uncertain).[13] What does remain low is public support for combat missions (33% in 2020, with an upward trend) and for arms exports even to friendly nations (30%).[14] Regardless of who occupies the chancellery in Berlin, consistent and sustained communication to engage the public in a conversation about the international challenges to their security and, more widely, the state the world is in, remains a deficit that should be addressed.

Military deployments abroad

As of April 2021, the Bundeswehr was deployed on 12 international operations involving a total of about 3,500 soldiers in Africa, Asia, Europe and the Middle East – less than 2% of the total active forces. Since the end of the Cold War, hundreds of thousands of German service personnel have served in some 50 operations, and the overall size of the German effort has varied with the ebb and flow of international crisis-management demands, in particular during the first decade of the 2000s when deployments peaked at 9,000–10,000 personnel.[15] While there certainly was lots of activity across a number of German governments during this period, little in terms of overall strategic narrative underpinned it.

During the mid- and late 1990s, both CDU-led and SPD governments framed crisis-management deployments in humanitarian and moral terms.[16] Leaders were furthermore motivated to demonstrate to partners that the newly unified Germany would be a reliable ally and a responsible foreign-policy actor.[17] Specific German national interests are usually gauged in a broader setting of international stability and humanitarian assistance. Even the deployment of special-operations forces in Afghanistan was described in parliamentary debates as effectively a police action rather than the pursuit of terrorists and insurgents.[18] The utility of force was not really explained in public during all these deployments, and where force was used it was described in as close to a civilian context as possible.

The employment of limited force-projection means for limited stabilisation and crisis-management ends lent itself to military symbolism. It cannot be denied that Germany did indeed participate in military crisis management. Germany's 'being there', although often determined to avoid combat operations, has been considered enough of a commitment for it to claim a vocal role among the troop-contributing nations in NATO, EU and some United Nations missions. Yet it has not been enough to make a strategic difference to those crises.

There is an interesting disjunction in this context between German politics and military practice, in that the Bundeswehr was very slow to adapt to the crisis-management paradigm in the 1990s and the 2000s. This was partly because political guidance continued to prioritise collective-defence operations until adjustments ushered in between 2003 and 2006, and partly because during and immediately following the Cold War the German armed forces were optimised for high-intensity combined-arms warfare. While the armed forces continued to train and equip themselves for this purpose, political and public discourse was focused on the argument that changes in the international security environment had made that very purpose obsolete. For the Bundeswehr that deployed to Afghanistan in 2002–03, the only active reference points (with the exception of some limited air-force missions against enemy air defences in the Kosovo campaign) were Cold War deterrence against the Eastern bloc and non-coercive Balkans peacekeeping focused on conflict mediation. Stabilisation operations and counter-insurgency tactics did not feature in Bundeswehr planning, which in part explains why the Bundeswehr initially struggled when the Northern insurgency in Afghanistan escalated from 2007–08 onwards. Training for core military skills was inspired by the Second World War, because the mission of armoured and mechanised infantry Bundeswehr units charged with defending Europe in the event of a Warsaw Pact invasion was not radically different from the German experience towards the end of the war.[19] The military skills on which the Bundeswehr remains based and that serve as the benchmark for many of the people serving in it are not acknowledged as desirable in public discourse to this day.

In generic functional terms, the spectrum of tasks for the armed forces ranges from peacetime activities to security and peacekeeping tasks, to combat and war fighting. In practice, Germany has tried to limit itself to the non-combat end of the spectrum. As former CDU defence minister Volker Rühe (with some palpable irritation) argued in 2019 with reference to the German habit of providing reconnaissance rather than combat aircraft for international operations, since 2005 'the Germans take the photos, the others are bombing – this is a special path that is not sustainable'.[20]

The larger point is that if military interventions are to be successful and contribute to the overall success of security-policy choices, the means deployed need to include those that are decisive in relation to the challenge at hand. Providing the political framework, as in the case of Germany's attempt to contribute to conflict resolution in Libya via the so-called 'Berlin Process', or only supportive and sometimes symbolic military assets – as, for example, in the case of Germany's involvement in the coalition to counter the Islamic State, also known as ISIS or ISIL – implies that Germany does not share the same risks that Berlin's partners accept, which is problematic for multi-lateral cohesion. It is also counterproductive, because it lowers the chances of interventions succeeding even if large amounts of political capital are invested. The particular ways in which Germany deploys the Bundeswehr – and the ways in which it does not – illustrate that armed force as an instrument of secu-rity policy has yet to be understood in its entirety: as a lever of national power to be employed in support of national strategy.

There is a debate within Germany concerning the modali-ties of parliamentary control over international deployments of the armed forces. This debate has been ongoing since 1994, when Germany's Federal Constitutional Court ruled that deployments outside NATO territory were constitutional but required parliamentary approval other than in emergency situations (when approval could be granted after the decision to deploy had been taken by the executive branch of govern-ment). The Bundestag must give consent prior to deployments and usually does so in the form of time-limited mandates in which deployment ceilings and the mission goal, as well as Bundeswehr tasks on the deployment, are defined. There is no evidence to suggest that the German armed forces are less likely to deploy or more likely to withdraw from a deployment because of this degree of parliamentary oversight. But the need to secure a parliamentary majority – and to do so repeatedly for longer-running missions – makes it likely that German deployments come with constraints and caveats, which, for example, caused concerns because of resulting limitations on the activities of German International Security Assistance Force (ISAF) troops in Afghanistan.[21] A commission led by Rühe reported in 2015 on how to maintain levels of parliamentary control while acknowledging that deeper and more varied integration of Bundeswehr elements into multinational formations and operations requires some rethinking of the rules to ensure that NATO and EU allies would have guaranteed access to the German assets and personnel pledged in case operations are called for. The issue remains unresolved and continues to be debated.[22] Ironically, the debates about parliamentary mandates for Bundeswehr missions represent the moments in which debate on security and defence matters actually reaches the public. But even this conversation, limited as it is, at its core concerns balancing national sovereignty (parliamentary control) with multinational requirements (pooling and sharing of capabilities) – not the purpose and utility of the armed forces in the pursuit of national interests and security-policy objectives.

Political guidance and the capability challenge of the Bundeswehr

In broad terms, Germany went from being a front-line state during the Cold War, to one of many European contributors to international military crisis-management efforts, to a country that struggles to define an overall ambition for its armed forces during a period in which the demands of territorial defence (for Germany in the form of collective defence in NATO), contributions to international security and crisis-management operations in an increasingly global context, and defence diplomacy and military assistance to civilian authorities simultaneously demand attention. While the task of managing a more complex and varied set of challenges is not unique to the Bundeswehr, Germany has, during three decades of adaptation, defence reform and attempts to provide political–military strategic guidance, managed to hollow out its armed forces to such a degree that, at the end of the Merkel era, their readiness and capability challenges have reached alarming proportions. In early 2021, Chief of Defence General Eberhard Zorn suggested that Germany will need 'to review [its] military goals', as declared to NATO and the EU, because the resources required to drive modernisation and increase readiness were higher than what had been budgeted.[23] A month later, news magazine *Der Spiegel* quoted from a classified planning document that 'many armament projects required to fulfil NATO-planning targets and EU-goals … cannot be implemented or initiated in time' because available resources simply do not allow it.[24] A few weeks later, the annual report of the parliamentary armed-forces commissioner suggested that there was little new to report on the 'current problems of the Bundeswehr: not enough equipment, not enough personnel, too much bureaucracy'.[25]

In 1994, a new German defence-strategy paper suggested that the core task of territorial defence should essentially remain unaffected by changes in the international security environment.[26] Military power projection for crisis-management purposes was at that point seen as neither desirable nor achievable by political and military leaders in Germany. Unfolding events in the Balkans and elsewhere nevertheless quickly underlined that the most likely missions the Bundeswehr might have to take on were crisis-management operations. Reform proposals of the early 2000s tried to grapple with this reality but did not resolve the tension. Instead, calls to improve the deployability of the armed forces so they could contribute to crisis management – which would affect their structure and equipment – sat alongside Germany's commitment to collective and territorial defence made in order to reassure itself and its allies that it would remain a reliable NATO member. A report issued in 2000 by then-defence minister Rudolf Scharping suggested that territorial and collective defence should be the primary guide for the size and structure of the German armed forces.[27] Scharping's successor, Peter Struck, like Scharping a social democrat, and influenced by the early stages of the Afghanistan deployment and policy papers drawn up by his staff at the defence ministry, pulled the German debate firmly in the direction of crisis-management operations, issuing defence-policy guidelines in 2003 that argued that capabilities maintained solely for conventional collective-defence tasks would no longer be required and that instead the structure of the Bundeswehr should be determined by crisis-management tasks.[28]

A white paper issued by the defence ministry in 2006, by then under Franz Josef Jung of the CDU, tried to fudge the question of priorities by arguing that, on the one hand, 'the central task of the Bundeswehr continues to be national and collective defence in the classical sense'. It continued on the same page to suggest that, on the other hand,

> for the foreseeable future, the most likely tasks will be the prevention of international conflicts and crisis management, to include the fight against international terrorism. They will determine the structure of and exert significant influence on the capabilities, command and control systems, availability, and equipment of the Bundeswehr.[29]

The German armed forces were left with an unsatisfactory middle ground in which the task deemed central was not the task that would drive capability development.

The most recent 'white book' national strategy paper – composed by then-defence minister Ursula von der Leyen, agreed by the cabinet and issued in 2016 – recognises the need to pursue several priorities simultaneously but essentially argues that national and collective defence, international crisis management, homeland security, defence diplomacy via partnership and cooperation, and humanitarian assistance are of 'equal importance'.[30] The analysis in the paper does emphasise territorial and collective defence within NATO, however, reflecting the deteriorating security environment in Europe, and concludes that a German contribution to deterrence must include the ability to engage in high-intensity combined-arms combat. It also suggests that, since future threats are likely to materialise in geographically contained areas and with little warning, the armed forces must improve their readiness and rapid-response capability.

Given that Germany does not have a national-security strategy document, white papers in particular serve to codify the state of the security and defence debate. However, their impact in terms of the broader public debate as well as defence planning is curiously limited. Sometimes contemporary events are unhelpful – the publication of the 2006 white paper was marred by revelations about the unsavoury behaviour of some of the German personnel deployed to Afghanistan, and the 2016 edition was caught up in the British referendum to leave the EU and the US election that would usher in Donald Trump's presidency – but such distractions cannot fully explain the lack of strategic impact. White papers are high-level strategy documents and their implications for capabilities and the structure of the armed forces are worked out and defined in lower-level documents that elaborate capability choices for the Bundeswehr in detail, even though, naturally, only part of their content will appear in the public domain. This work does happen, and it is often very clear-eyed, coherent and undertaken with a long-term perspective in mind.

Germany's main area of underperformance over the past ten to 15 years has not been a failure to translate broad strategic ambition into an understanding of that ambition's military prerequisites in terms of capability profiles. Rather, the failure has been the inability to generate the support to unlock the resources required to fund the implementation of these military capabilities: there has been insufficient political acceptance of what is actually needed to enact these ambitions. As a result, the gap between what is required and what is available has widened across all major indicators: military readiness, personnel, procurement and defence spending.

The readiness issues, the delays in procurement, the difficulties of getting new equipment to operational status and structural underfunding are all well-rehearsed and debated publicly, with analytical judgements suggesting that the Bundeswehr's readiness, if measured in the context of the core task of collective defence, has reached historical lows.[31] The German parliamentary commissioner for the armed forces regularly publishes reports on operational readiness and equipment availability that paint a bleak picture. In a report published in January 2020, covering 2019, the commissioner argued that while 'there are intense political efforts to improve operational readiness', these had not translated into effective action: 'the troops are still not really noticing the "trend reversals" that have been initiated … Old structures and processes that have long since ceased to be expedient mean that all too many efforts are amounting to nothing.' On the operational status of major weapons systems, the commissioner suggested '100 per cent equipment, weapons, ammunition, personal equipment and reliable system readiness' were required but 'the Bundeswehr is still a long way from achieving this … Everything is progressing too sluggishly.'[32]

Senior German officers have defined a clear path forward, both in terms of national defence planning and in a multinational setting via the NATO Defence Planning Process (NDPP). The 2018 Bundeswehr Concept (*Konzeption der Bundeswehr*) makes clear that the German armed forces can only hope to be able to deal with the varied and rapidly changing security environment if they are fully equipped, fully trained and fully manned. In 2017, Erhard Bühler, then the director general for planning in the defence ministry, was quoted publicly as having identified 'substantial need for adjustment for the Bundeswehr in all possible temporal and functional facets'.[33] Core aspects of German promises in the NDPP during 2017 were to rebuild the German army to provide three fully digitised combat divisions, with a total of eight to ten brigades by 2032. Milestones to this plan were identified as a fully equipped and combat-ready brigade in 2023 and a division by 2027. Targets for a surface and subsurface fleet in the navy were agreed and the air force was given the ambition of leading a multinational force capable of flying some 350 combat missions, some 250–60 of which would be flown by German aircraft. In other words, in 2017 and 2018 the main military and defence-planning decisions, seeking to implement the political–strategic guidance enshrined in the 2016 white paper, were interpreted within multinational processes.[34] In 2020, Zorn argued that, while no longer a front-line state, German territory remained crucial to enable the rapid movement of allied forces and, as an operational rear area, was a likely target within range of direct strikes by opponents. He stressed that the Bundeswehr would need to be prepared for high-intensity combat and be fully equipped and ready during peacetime to be a credible deterrent.[35]

While military leaders have provided fairly clear guidance regarding the purposes and requirements of the armed forces, the requisite funding has not always been forthcoming. Lt-Gen. Alfons Mais, the army chief, argued in February 2021 that the army's guiding principle should be the requirement to prevail in combat against a capable opponent, and that this required the force to be fully equipped with modern equipment across its three divisions. Germany would need to be able to operate at division level again to contribute to deterring Russia with conventional means and serving as a framework nation for partners, thus providing the command-and-control and enabling capability that could integrate smaller allies.[36] Mais's assessment indicated that achieving this goal was some way off: the brigade that is scheduled to serve as the NATO Very High Readiness Joint Task Force land component in 2023 will again have to borrow some equipment from sister units to be appropriately equipped. The same issues, although on an even larger scale, had also plagued the unit that had assumed this task in 2019. Germany will also have to wait until at least 2027 for software-defined radios to become more widely available in the Bundeswehr. Currently, Mais explained, Germany's partners have to switch their modern systems into emergency mode – in other words, downgrade their capability – so that the Bundeswehr, the framework nation, can achieve interoperability. Mais identified the defence of deployed personnel against a variety of threats from the air as a particularly glaring capability gap.

When Lt-Gen. Ingo Gerhartz had completed his set of initial visits in 2018 after being appointed chief of the air force, he concluded that the air force had reached a 'low point'.[37] In early 2021, feeling more upbeat, Gerhartz argued that the air force was 'upgrading its assets to bring it up into the pinnacle of today's military aviation capabilities'.[38] However, the flagship project for a Future Combat Air System (FCAS), which includes a new fighter aircraft as well as other air assets and weapons systems, pursued with France and Spain, had encountered significant turbulence, putting the project at risk; a replacement decision for the ageing *Tornado* platform had yet to be taken despite being overdue; the question of whether or not Germany should purchase armed uninhabited aerial vehicles (UAVs) remained unresolved after more than a decade of debate; and procurement plans to replace CH-53G heavy transport helicopters with a modern platform were put on hold in 2020.

In January 2021, the outgoing navy chief, Vice Admiral Andreas Krause, argued that after 25 years of reductions and shrinkage, the navy's task was now to grow again in what he termed 'the most comprehensive modernisation in [its] history'.[39] In 2020, Krause referred to Germany's various naval tasks – including its obligations in the Baltic Sea (where Germany is an important maritime actor), securing sea lines of communication in the North Atlantic, maritime-security operations in the Mediterranean, and helping to secure maritime trade routes in the Indian Ocean – and noted that the navy was assuming 'the most comprehensive task spectrum of its history with the smallest fleet of its history. For the foreseeable future we will not have operational reserves.'[40] He explained that the navy had to modernise and grow at the same time as discharging its responsibilities, which he characterised as being global, and would need to rebuild its capacity for multidimensional naval warfare, including anti-submarine warfare, and the ability to command and control larger operations.

The purpose of German military power that lies behind the ideas that military leaders have circulated for almost five years, but which political leaders have not embraced or communicated effectively to the public, is to be a major pillar of European defence capability in NATO and the EU, focused primarily, but not exclusively, on land forces. Thinking about contingencies beyond the European continent is understandably more pronounced in the navy and the air force, with both services planning temporary deployments to the Indo-Pacific region in 2021 and 2022 respectively.[41]

The political debate about defence policy in Germany – and often about Germany in other countries – focuses on the '2%-of-GDP on defence' metric featured in the 2014 NATO defence investment pledge. Very rarely, if at all, do leaders explain why, precisely, more money is required or what 'doing more' translates into in specific capability but also responsibility terms. The capability goals that the national defence-planning process and the NDPP have proposed for Germany would return the Bundeswehr to a role that is not very different – even though the context has changed significantly – from what it used to be: a central building block of the conventional defence of NATO. Achieving this would be an important step: it would strengthen the ability of Europeans to deter and defend against Russia and would lighten some of the burden the US carries in Europe. This step needs to be complemented by the reali-sation that Germany also needs to think about its military contribution to constraining China. The two tasks are linked – the most significant role Germany can play in the latter is by creating credible capabilities to deter Russia and, if neces-sary, to defend NATO and EU member-state territory against Russian incursions. Europeans, who over the course of the next ten years must create the ability to defend themselves at home, will notably reduce US obligations in Europe just at the point when China hopes to be able to challenge comprehen-sively US military dominance in the Asia-Pacific. Conducting security operations in the extended European periphery, in the Mediterranean, the Indian Ocean and Africa, will help to quell sources of instability and risks to European security, but will also establish a European footprint in regions of the world in which China is increasing its own presence and thus demonstrate a willingness to contest Beijing's strategic expan-sion. Contributing assets, even in limited form, for security tasks and missions in the Indo-Pacific will furthermore signal to Germany's partners there, and to the US, that Berlin accepts responsibility for global order and acknowledges their security concerns in deed and word.

Defence spending

Germany's underfunding of its armed forces has created a readiness and credibility gap at the heart of the transatlantic alliance. The amount Germany spends on defence is determined by a political bargaining process, constrained by economic indicators and outlook, and driven by threat perceptions, as well as existing and expected commitments. There is no structural reason why Germany currently spends less than 2% of GDP (the NATO recommendation), just as there is no structural reason that would make 2% of GDP – an arbitrary target as such – the right amount. In 1980, West Germany spent about 2.7% of its GDP on defence; in 1990 still 2.4%. This declined further to 1.5% in 2000 and 1.2% in 2010.[42] A temporary low was reached in 2014–16 when it hovered around 1.1%, although since then spending has increased and reached just under 1.4% of GDP in 2020. In defence-investment terms, Germany directed 15–20% of defence spending to weapons procurement and research and development in the 2010s, whereas allies such as France, the UK or the US can be expected to spend 20–30% on this category. Germany does spend quite a lot on defence: its defence budget stood at €44.9 billion in 2020, which puts it comfortably among the top-ten spenders worldwide.[43] And yet this is not enough to finance the capability ambition that Germany declared in NATO and that its defence planners have outlined. The most important question is not whether one spends more than in the past but whether one spends enough to meet the challenge.

While there is some justified criticism of the 2% NATO spending target, curious additional reasons are sometimes advanced to argue against increased German spending. One

Figure 1: **Germany's defence budget, 2008–20**

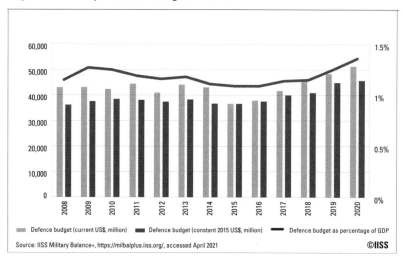

Source: IISS Military Balance+, https://milbalplus.iiss.org/, accessed April 2021 ©IISS

is to suggest that the Bundeswehr would not know what to do with more money; another is to suggest that the defence ministry and the armed forces would not have the technical capacity to absorb significant additional financial outlays.[44]

The former point is not credible. Merkel, speaking about defence spending, said at the 2019 Munich Security Conference that 'of course, we must also ask ourselves what we're doing with this money'.[45] The capability targets set in 2017 and 2018, discussed above, have identifiable costs that defence and military officials have communicated to the political leadership. As Brig.-Gen. (Retd) Rainer Meyer zum Felde suggested, internal defence ministry assumptions were based on defence spending levels of €58bn–60bn by 2024 and 2025, with a simultaneous doubling of the spending on defence investment.[46] However, following the federal elections of 2017, which returned the CDU/CSU–SPD grand coalition to power, none of the financial-planning documents, which are agreed annually on a rolling basis and currently stretch to 2025, reflected these numbers. Ministry of Defence planning documents leaked in early 2021 suggested that an additional €9bn would be required in 2022, €15.9bn more in 2024 and an additional €20.7bn in 2026 to meet the declared capability objectives, whereas finance-ministry planning assumptions forecast a defence-budget decline between 2022 and 2025.[47] There is a long list of important looming procurement decisions that government budgets do not currently financially support: air and missile defence; land-forces digitisation; *Tornado* replacement; an interim solution for P-3C *Orion* maritime-patrol-aircraft replacement; Eurofighter evolution; support helicopters; airborne intelligence, surveillance and reconnaissance (ISR); additional *Puma* infantry fighting vehicle (IFV) orders; replacement of heavy transport helicopters; additional satellite communications; *Boxer* armoured-vehicle upgrades; and *Tiger* attack-helicopter evolution.[48]

The second criticism – about the technical capacity to absorb additional financial outlays – is somewhat more credible because the German procurement and acquisition process remains slow and inefficient, often producing outcomes that are delayed, are over budget and generate less capability than planned (see Chapter Three). The Bundesrechnungshof (the federal auditing office) has repeatedly exposed waste and inefficiencies, and occasionally the defence ministry does not manage to spend the money it has been allocated for a given financial year, usually because of issues with large procurement projects.[49] Bureaucracy, industry and politics have all contributed to this situation.

To create a higher degree of sustained political commitment towards defence-planning ambitions and particularly the long-term financial implications of planning decisions, Rühe has argued that Germany needs the equivalent of the French military planning law,[50] a piece of legislation that provides a multi-year financial framework to enable implementation of national and multinational capability targets and that removes this funding – to a degree – from the ebb and flow of party politics. The idea was amplified by several analysts and in 2020 also featured in a speech by Minister of Defence Kramp-Karrenbauer, who argued that it was a good idea to follow the example of other European states in this area.[51]

More than 20 years after Germany first participated in an official combat mission (*Operation Allied Force* in 1999), the debate about and use of the military instrument as a tool of national strategy and policy remains stunted. To be sure, there has been gradual adaptation over time and many an earlier taboo (including out-of-area operations, combat operations as part of crisis management, and supplying arms to parties in active conflict) has fallen by the wayside as history marched on. However, in a world in which significant players, including all the major powers, see continued utility in the use of armed force for foreign-policy objectives, Germany's political leaders need to go further and initiate a more honest conversation with the public: on the purpose of armed force in international crisis-management operations and interventions; on the function of the armed forces and the essence of their task, which remains the ability to prevail in combat; and on the costs of funding the armed forces at a level that would allow them to achieve the tasks set out in strategy documents.

CHAPTER THREE

Defence procurement, technology and industry

Military capability and defence output more widely reflect the choices – political, financial, military and societal – that nations make. Defence planners everywhere face a fundamental dilemma in the current international security environment: those with too narrow a focus will be vulnerable to surprise and will struggle to adapt, while those trying to prepare for every possible threat will find their resources wanting. Intensifying great-power competition is occurring under digitised conditions. Access to very-capable and very-lethal weapons systems continues to spread. The pace of innovation continues to accelerate, and innovation that is relevant for defence increasingly occurs in segments of the private sector that have few or no previous connections to defence. New technology – in such areas as artificial intelligence (AI), big data and robotics – will change the way nations fight. Armed forces of the future will field a mix of crewed, uninhabited and autonomous capabilities or risk being seriously disadvantaged. Military practitioners have noted that it would be extremely challenging to respond to a combination of precision strikes and cyber attacks, amplified by orchestrated social-media misinformation campaigns targeting Western nations.[1] So beyond rebuilding armed forces for conventional operations, which will remain important, the more transformational challenge entails examining how to achieve military effect from a distance and strengthening resilience at home while weakening the societal resilience of opponents. The core of command-and-control arrangements will be increasingly digital, which in turn will influence how future capabilities will be employed.[2]

Governments therefore need to make difficult and important choices: about how to maintain or rebuild military capabilities that can deal with the world as it is, and invest in the technology and the capacity to prepare for a future that will differ from the present. For the armed forces to be a useful instrument of government policy, they need to be equipped correctly, benefit from innovation and modern technology (not to replace strategy or doctrine but to enable it), and be able to draw upon a defence-industrial base that delivers world-class products. Agile procurement, a strong defence-innovation ecosystem – the network of companies, research organisations and government agencies that cooperate and compete in a number of technology areas – and a capable defence-industrial base are indispensable elements of military capability.

Germany, at the end of the Merkel era, is not well positioned to make these choices and deliver the military capabilities required to meet the challenges it faces. If left unchanged, a major implication of this situation is that future German governments will have fewer political opportunities to influence and even shape strategic challenges and their solutions. Some principles that worked in the past will continue to be relevant despite changing circumstances. They include, for example, to be fully equipped even in peacetime; to maintain sufficient spares and a capacity to repair and overhaul equipment; to train often, at scale and with challenging and realistic scenarios; and to make sure that those responsible for achieving the Bundeswehr missions have some control over the resources made available to do so. None of these principles are currently met.

The Bundeswehr does not receive – and has not received for some time – the modern equipment it needs when it needs it. What it does receive is often late, more expensive and somewhat less capable than originally envisioned. While many defence-modernisation efforts of NATO and EU member states also struggle to be on time and on budget, Germany's situation is particularly troubling. In September 2020, procurement plans for new heavy transport helicopters were halted because the way in which requirements were refined made it impossible to acquire the helicopters within the available budget parameters. In October 2020, an order for assault rifles that had already been awarded was cancelled because of irregularities in the procurement process. The following month, budget allocations for an air- and missile-defence system were so low that industry partners indicated that they might need to reconsider their position in Germany. Further examples underline that Germany's procurement process is both overly bureaucratic and underperforming.[3] Germany is currently badly positioned to build forces that are ready for modern operations. This situation undermines the Bundeswehr's ability to operate effectively and in coordination with partners and allies, and it raises costs in areas that then themselves become obstacles to future-oriented defence investment spending, given the escalating costs of keeping legacy equipment in service. This downward spiral informs analyses that the Bundeswehr is currently unfit for purpose.[4]

The policy debate about major procurement decisions, the processes and the implications of defence innovation and technology, and the defence industry and arms exports reflects the nature of domestic institutions, the absence of a positive and accepted vision for the future of the Bundeswehr as an instrument of German foreign and security policy, and the tactical political manoeuvres that this absence has engendered. As a result, Germany is at risk of further eroding its military capability, losing interoperability with core partners in NATO and the EU, and weakening a defence-technology and -industrial base that has traditionally been able to design and manufacture equipment to meet requirements across all military domains. Furthermore, defence-relevant advanced technologies that originate in the civilian realm are increasingly proliferating worldwide. The disruptive potential of some of these technologies – AI, machine learning, miniaturisation, automation and robotics, to name a few – for international stability and the future character of conflict is considerable. Continuing on the path Berlin has trod for the previous decade or so would gradually erode not just whatever technological advantage a well-equipped Bundeswehr would enjoy when called upon to perform, but also the political options and choices available to future German chancellors.

The defence-procurement conundrum

Some German defence-modernisation and procurement decisions have proven disadvantageous, whereas on other issues a decision has simply not been made, with dire consequences for German defence policy and capability. In 2010, then-defence minister Karl-Theodor zu Guttenberg, almost in passing, introduced a paradigm shift for defence planning that would have lasting consequences. During a speech at the Bundeswehr Command and Staff College in Hamburg, in an attempt to grapple with the budget pressures generated by the financial and economic crisis of 2008–09, the minister effectively suggested that defence-planning assumptions should be guided by a design-to-cost approach rather than the traditional cost-to-design framework, and indicated that he would be willing to cut several billion euros from the defence budgets of the coming years.[5]

While zu Guttenberg's remarks must be understood within the context of preparing wide-ranging structural changes that ultimately led to a smaller Bundeswehr and the suspension of conscription in 2011, the paradigm shift is notable. It implied that the size of the defence budget would not be driven by an assessment of threats and challenges and the political level of ambition of the government that is then translated into military requirements, funded through the defence budget; but rather that the military level of ambition would be defined by an amount of money set before that assessment is performed. Within a month of zu Guttenberg's speech, the cabinet decided to cut €8.3 billion from the defence budget between 2011 and 2014 (later extended to 2015), equivalent to around 6% of expenditure.[6] Financial realities generally tend to be a constraining factor on any state's defence ambitions and hardly any defence-modernisation plan is drawn up in ignorance of the financial settlement that is likely achievable in a given political context. However, it is rare for a defence minister to volunteer such cuts and to change the decision-making framework to a primarily budget-led defence policy.[7]

A central pillar of the Bundeswehr modernisation plan agreed at the end of 2010 and launched in 2011 by zu Guttenberg's successor, Thomas de Maizière, was to try to maintain as broad a capability spectrum as possible while accepting constraints on sustainability – Breite vor Tiefe (roughly 'breadth before depth') was the associated slogan at the time.[8] Avoiding a prioritisation of capability areas that would have implied a cut of complete equipment programmes and certain force roles might have been in part intended to help soothe

the armed forces and reconcile them to the reduced-resource environment.[9] However, it also contributed to the readiness challenge the armed forces now face, with, for example, cuts to maintenance capacity and spare parts and greater dependency on the private sector for maintenance, repair and overhaul resulting from these decisions.

At the time, German decision-makers also interpreted the security environment as calling for a reassessment of requirements, which led in 2012 and 2013 to the reduction of the order size of several equipment programmes that were intended to replace legacy equipment in the armed forces. Cutbacks included a reduced order of the *Tiger* attack helicopter (from 80 to 57), the NH90 helicopter (from 122 to 82) and the *Puma* infantry fighting vehicle (IFV, from 405 to 350).[10] The order for the A400M transport plane was also reduced in 2010 (from 60 to 53), although this was also influenced by the overall restructuring of the programme and of the contract between customer nations and industry, alongside shifting requirements.[11]

From a cost-control perspective, it must be acknowledged that all the programmes mentioned above experienced a significant degree of cost escalation over time. An external consulting report commissioned by the Ministry of Defence in 2014 suggested that large armaments projects in Germany suffered from weaknesses in the acquisition process – including contract design and insufficient risk- and project-management capacity – which contributed to delays, quality problems and cost increases.[12] Germany's procurement cycle, like that of other NATO nations, is marked by delays, and contracts would normally include price-escalation clauses to cover rising costs and inflation throughout the research-and-development, production and delivery phases. In addition, given the long lead times that characterise traditional defence procurement (when not driven by urgent operational requirements), technological advances occurring during the procurement process will most likely need to be integrated, which will carry costs. Failure to implement early design freezes frequently create add-on requirements generated by the customer, resulting in additional costs. As a programme thus moves from development to production and active service, the unit cost inevitably increases, potentially creating tipping points where a reduction in volume is a likely cost-control measure, as has been the case in Germany.

Industry also contributed to the unsatisfactory situation in several cases by not delivering as expected. Germany originally ordered the *Puma* IFV in 2009 to replace the *Marder*, a vehicle that has been in Bundeswehr service since 1971.[13] The *Puma* programme has been marred by technical difficulties, including low-quality initial production runs, and will not reach its full operating capability before the late 2020s.[14] As a result, the *Marder* has received, and continues to receive, numerous upgrades,[15] and is being kept in the fleet for much longer than anticipated. This creates a maintenance challenge because of obsolete and ageing spare parts. In the maritime dimension, the successor for the *Bremen*-class frigate, the F125 *Baden-Württemberg* class, was ordered in 2007.[16] While the first *Baden-Württemberg* class was due to be commissioned in 2014, this was postponed due to delays in construction and problems identified during trials with the navy, including an overall weight that was heavier than expected and badly balanced – a serious design flaw – and electronics, radars and even the flameproof coating were found wanting. After initial trials, the ship was deemed unseaworthy by the navy and returned to its builders to remedy these issues. The *Baden-Württemberg* finally commissioned into service in mid-2019, with the second of its class following in 2020.[17] One of the implications of this delay is, again, that the old *Bremen*-class frigates had to be kept in service for longer than planned at significant cost.

As of early 2021, the German government must make several procurement decisions to replace ageing equipment and close capability gaps. The assets in question range from heavy transport helicopters to replace the CH-53G, to new submarines, to air and missile defence, to intelligence, surveillance and reconnaissance (ISR) programmes. It is, however, the replacement for the *Tornado* aircraft that has become more of a political football than any of the other programmes.

The *Tornado*, which entered the Bundeswehr inventory in 1981, is used by Germany in the fighter/ground-attack and electronic-warfare roles, but also for delivering tactical nuclear weapons under NATO's dual-capable aircraft (DCA) arrangement. Currently, the plan foresees the *Tornado* withdrawn from active service between 2025 and 2030, which is already later than originally intended, but extension to 2035 is being mooted.[18] The government has declared that it intends to provide a seamless transition to a new airframe or airframes without interruption to any of the *Tornado* roles, including nuclear. In 2020, the defence ministry declared that it intends to procure a mixed-fleet solution with Eurofighter aircraft and the F/A-18F *Super Hornet* and EA-18G *Growler,* having in 2019 ruled out purchases of the F-15 and the F-35, the other aircraft originally considered. To turn this intention into a commitment, the government needs to formally introduce supporting documents for the procurement into parliamentary debate; this step is envisioned for 2022 or 2023.

The Ministry of Defence approach represents a compromise between capability requirements and NATO Defence Planning Process (NDPP) commitments, defence-industrial interests and alliance management. While the *Tornado* clearly needs to be replaced, pursuing an F-35 purchase, as some officers in the Bundeswehr had preferred on capability grounds, would be a blow to the German and European defence industry. A mixed-fleet solution like the one proposed presents some operational advantages (such as flexibility and the option to replace systems successively) but also recognises that the Eurofighter is not currently certified for the use of US-owned and -controlled nuclear weapons, nor does it have the required electronic-warfare capabilities.[19] Buying the intended mix of Eurofighter, *Super Hornet* and *Growler* aircraft also protects existing plans for a Franco-German Future Combat Air System (FCAS). This is because the in-service life and development potential of the Eurofighter and the F/A-18 will be more limited than that of the F-35 would be. Thus, the mixed-fleet solution provides an opportunity for Germany to channel a notable contract to US industry after a time in which German–US relations had become strained, but without undermining the industrial rationale for a new European combat air-development project.

The nuclear role of the *Tornado* – and its replacement – has provided an additional layer of complexity and puts further pressure on the decision-making timeline. Germany, like several other European NATO states, hosts several dozen US tactical nuclear weapons – the B-61, a gravity bomb designed to be dropped directly on enemy positions. These weapons are under US control but would be released for use by German aircraft during a conflict. During the Cold War, it was hoped that such an arrangement would enhance the credibility of nuclear deterrence against Warsaw Pact forces, without states such as Germany having to acquire nuclear weapons themselves. According to media reports, the Bundesrechnungshof (Germany's federal audit office) assumes that it will cost some €7.7bn to keep the *Tornado* flying until 2030, a cost that would rise to €10.2bn if that timeline is pushed back to 2035. Those reports also suggested that the US Department of Defense indicated that nuclear certification for the F/A-18 could be achieved by 2027–30 if Germany indicated in 2020 that it wanted to proceed, whereas nuclear certification for the Eurofighter would take an additional two to five years, thus pushing the timeline to 2029–35, while also being more expensive.[20] Given that Germany did not make a commitment in 2020, there is a risk that further delays to the decision-making process would interrupt Germany's ability to fulfil its NATO DCA role.

Some Germans might find such an outcome desirable. The *Tornado* replacement decision has become entangled in the question of whether Germany should remain in NATO's nuclear club through its ability to deliver US tactical nuclear weapons. The CDU/CSU–FDP coalition led by Merkel in 2009–13 was based on a coalition agreement that stated, 'we will advocate within the Alliance and with our American allies the removal of the remaining nuclear weapons from Germany'.[21] Then-foreign minister Guido Westerwelle (FDP) was particularly keen to pursue this ambition, and the coalition agreement at the time also made references to the vision of a world free of nuclear weapons that then-US president Barack Obama had promoted. On the other hand, the 2018 coalition agreement between the CDU/CSU and SPD for the term that ends in September 2021 suggests that it is in Germany's interest to participate in NATO's nuclear-planning processes and discussions for as long as nuclear weapons are part of NATO's strategic concept. While also endorsing the goal of a nuclear-weapons-free world, it links a removal of US tactical nuclear-weapons to the precondition of successful nuclear disarmament and arms control.[22] Thus, arguably, given wider strategic developments, such as a notable erosion of the arms-control environment that includes the demise of the 1987 Intermediate-Range Nuclear Forces (INF) Treaty, alongside the nuclear-modernisation ambitions of the main nuclear-weapons powers, that precondition is not being met. SPD co-chairman Norbert Walter-Borjans, however, declared that he was against Germany's nuclear role and therefore also against replacing those *Tornado*s that are designated for the DCA arrangement. Others in the SPD disagree with him – as do prominent CDU/CSU members of parliament – but their position has been weakened as a result of a series of resignations in the face of a recent push to a more left-leaning direction pursued by Walter-Borjans, his co-chair Saskia Esken and the chairman of the SPD parliamentary group, Rolf Mützenich.[23] Overall, the *Tornado* saga exemplifies the wider challenge: Germany's ability to procure at the scale and speed required is hampered by a lack of financial resources, an inefficient and in parts ineffective procurement process, and wavering political support.

Technology, innovation and their responsible use in defence

The 2020 edition of the Global Innovation Index ranks Germany among the top ten most innovative economies in the world, a spot it has held consistently in recent years.[24] While Germany is good at innovating for wider economic gain, studies of defence innovation have found it to be 'reluctant to innovate in the pursuit of military advantage' and unwilling to look 'to leverage private-sector innovation to improve its armed forces and attain offsetting capabilities'.[25] While this may present an obstacle to rapid defence innovation and to fully exploiting the potential of technology, in Germany ethical, moral and legal constraints are routinely balanced against imperatives generated by security or industrial policy. It has been argued that the German debate tends to apply old concepts and notions of, for example, arms control to new technologies such as cyber and AI.[26] But this tendency is not the result of a failure to recognise that change is under way and new technologies are proliferating – rather, it reflects the policy preferences of many Germans and their elected officials.

This particular setting can itself generate novel and innovative approaches. For example, to accompany the development of the FCAS, Airbus, together with the Fraunhofer Institute for Communication, Information Processing and Ergonomics (FKIE), part of the government-owned applied-science research organisation Fraunhofer-Gesellschaft, established an expert commission on the responsible use of technology in the FCAS. Given that AI, big-data analytics and human–machine interfaces, among other technologies, will all play a role in the FCAS, the commission – which is explicitly and directly supported by the government and seeks to involve a wide range of societal stakeholders in its conversation – is meant to debate the following question:

> How can we ensure that we develop a European air defence system that meets the mission requirements of the 21st century on a global scale, while at the same time guaranteeing that the system is under the full control of a responsible human operator at all times and whatever the circumstances?

The innovative idea of this forum is to implement a large-scale future defence project that is built on 'ethical and legal compliance by design' and seek to achieve this by leading a multi-stakeholder dialogue that includes civil-society and research actors who are known to hold sceptical views when it comes to armaments research and the use of military force.[27] What kind of proposals and possibly even guidelines or rules emerge from this process remains to be seen, but it is telling that this initiative started in Germany, where ethical and legal constraints were perhaps perceived by industry to be higher than in France, the other main partner nation in FCAS, or Spain, which joined the FCAS project in 2019.

Since 2019, under the leadership of Foreign Minister Heiko Maas (SPD), Germany has convened several international conferences and expert workshops on the relationship between new and emerging technologies and arms control.[28] One of the themes debated in this framework in 2020, and related to the idea pursued in the FCAS forum, was to explore how actors in science and technology from areas that might not be primarily military but have militarily relevant applications can be made more aware of the defence and arms-control implications of the innovations driving their fields.[29] The German government has embarked on an entrepreneurial approach to norm development when it comes to the responsible use of new technologies in defence and has tried to create a broad basis of support for its ideas both in Germany and internationally. Ultimately, the aim of this approach might be summarised as defining reliable limits to the application of certain technologies in weapons systems. The involvement of civil-society and non-governmental organisations – often with well-trained advocacy teams and clearly articulated positions sceptical of the armed forces – is ultimately intended to generate consensus and produce a higher level of acceptance of defence applications of dual-use technology. However, there is little evidence that this approach works – for example, the debate about providing the German armed forces with armed uninhabited aerial vehicles (UAVs) has been raging for around a decade and the positions remain largely unchanged: one camp fears the prospect of unaccountable killer robots, whereas the other sees the need to fill a glaring capability gap.

Beyond the challenge of defining the rules of the road, however, ultimately is the equally important challenge of how to support and enable defence innovation that ensures the Bundeswehr has access to world-leading technology and equipment so that it can meet its capability requirements, deal with the future character of conflict, remain interoperable with allies and avoid putting its own soldiers at unreasonable risk when on operations. While technological innovation has long been perceived as a means to achieve competitiveness and also a degree of national autonomy in defence-industrial terms, until recently defence innovation in Germany did not benefit from the kind of dedicated structures, technology incubators or strategies that other countries, in particular the US, have adopted. Berlin has more recently invested resources in this area by establishing the Bundeswehr Cyber Innovation Hub (CIH) in 2016, the Centre for Digitisation and Technology Research at the Bundeswehr universities in Hamburg and Munich (dtec.bw) in 2020, the Federal Agency for Disruptive Innovation (SPRIND) in 2019 and a cyber-security agency in 2020. Between them they are meant to drive digitisation, import a start-up culture to government-driven innovation and build relationships with the start-up community, and enable technological leapfrogging – in other words to innovate faster and to do so as unburdened as is legally possible by standard government procurement and research-and-development practices. While CIH is an agency of the armed forces and dtec.bw an academic Bundeswehr research centre, the other two are not; and SPRIND, funded by the Ministry of Education and Research and the Ministry for Economic Affairs and Energy, is explicitly civilian, with little appetite to cross over into defence applications. While it remains to be seen whether these new elements of the German innovation ecosystem will produce a lasting effect, in particular for defence innovation, they do represent a much more systematic approach to confronting the challenge of rapid innovation across a number of technologies.[30]

Technology and its defence application have, however, become very politicised in Germany on occasion, with detrimental effects for defence capabilities. The most prominent example is the abovementioned debate about whether the Bundeswehr should arm its UAVs. While the capabilities of systems of this kind vary, they have proliferated worldwide. As of 2020, at least 24 countries had some form of armed UAV in active service in their inventories, according to IISS data (see Table 1), and at least another six had either recently signed combat-UAV procurement contracts or were preparing to do so. While the US, long the dominant actor in this field, had exercised restraint in exporting this kind of equipment, China and Turkey have recently emerged as significant exporters.

Table 1: **Armed UAV operators in 2020 (active service)**

Operator country	Supplier nations
Algeria	China; UAE
Azerbaijan	Turkey
China	China
Egypt	China
France	United States
Indonesia	China
Iran	Iran
Iraq	China
Israel	Types unknown
Jordan	China
Kazakhstan	China
Myanmar	China
Nigeria	China
Pakistan	China
Qatar	Turkey
Saudi Arabia	China
Serbia	China
Sudan	China
Turkey	Turkey
Turkmenistan	China
Ukraine	Turkey
United Arab Emirates (UAE)	China
United Kingdom	United States
United States	United States

Source: IISS Military Balance+, https://milbalplus.iiss.org/, accessed April 2021

The German armed forces operate light, medium and heavy UAVs for ISR missions; as of early 2021, all of them are unarmed. In 2018, Germany signed an operator agreement with Airbus for the lease of five *Heron* TP UAVs, which are produced by the company Israel Aerospace Industries (IAI) and are likely to enter active Bundeswehr service in 2022 (the Bundeswehr is already operating *Heron* 1 UAVs, including on operations in Afghanistan and Mali). The lease arrangement is meant to bridge the capability gap until a European system has been developed.

While the capability gap is recognised, including the force-protection value such systems would afford deployed Bundeswehr personnel, various ethical, legal and moral arguments are advanced against a procurement decision. These arguments tend to conflate uninhabited and remotely controlled assets with fully autonomous and automated systems that might, according to some, lead to a greater willingness to use force. While it appeared in 2020 as if the governing coalition was finally ready to make a decision, several SPD leaders walked away from this consensus, demanding further debate and reflection. As commentators have observed, with 2021 being an election year, some SPD leaders might be tempted to attempt to generate political support by refusing to proceed with the procurement decision – playing to the political base on this issue and on defence spending featured in the 2013 and 2017 campaigns. While those approaches were not very successful politically, repeating this tactic in 2021 would undermine Bundeswehr capability.[31]

Germany remains reluctant to pursue technological innovation for the purpose of getting better at fighting wars. Political and societal constraints define boundaries to acceptable behaviour – in ethical and moral terms, perhaps also legal – that are not shared by other actors, both allies and opponents. In extreme cases, as in the armed-UAV debate, the implications are that the German armed forces suffer from a well-documented and widely recognised capability gap: in this case one that puts Germany's own deployed personnel at greater than necessary risk.

Defence industry and arms exports

Germany – alongside France, Italy, Norway, Spain, Sweden and the UK – is one of the major defence-industrial players in Europe. According to the German security- and defence-industry association BDSV, the sector directly accounts for some 135,000 jobs in Germany and a value creation of some €12bn annually.[32] Its defence industry is privately owned but not necessarily listed. Only three German companies appeared in the Defense News Top 100 list in 2020, which ranks companies by defence-related revenue: Rheinmetall, Hensoldt and Diehl.[33]

Aside from equipping the armed forces and contributing to a state's innovation capacity, armaments policy is also related to national political autonomy, securing technological skills and jobs, accessing international markets, and building alliances and partnerships. German armaments policy is marked by a desire to strengthen the wider European defence-industrial base. Compared to other European countries, Germany is less focused on national autonomy and seeks more international collaboration but, in tension with those goals, pursues a comparatively restrictive arms-export approach.

A strategy paper released by the German federal government in 2020 states that the defence industry is a strategically relevant factor for security, defence, technology and industrial policy. It describes security-relevant information technology and communications, AI, surface and underwater naval shipbuilding, command and control for network-enabled operations and crypto, protected and armoured vehicles, and sensors and electronic warfare as key capabilities and capacities that should be maintained at the national level. For other defence-industrial areas, notably military aerospace and air and missile defence, the government accepts a degree of dependency on European or global suppliers. The paper does not detail where, if at all, the lines between European and wider international dependencies should be drawn. Cooperation and integration in Europe are considered to offer the advantages of increased military interoperability and defence-industrial competitiveness and the potential for economic synergies.[34] The main messages of the paper are that the defence industry is a strategic asset and one that, in order to thrive, should exploit opportunities for European collaboration. The unacknowledged weakness of this position is that it is only sustainable if Germany's position on international armaments exports is relaxed.

Nearly all the procurement decisions for major weapons systems that are awaiting approval in Germany involve some form of international collaboration at the governmental or industrial level. The most significant in terms of future ambition is the Franco-German partnership. The Treaty of Aachen, signed by France and Germany on the 56th anniversary of the Elysée Treaty on 22 January 2019, provides an important indicator of the state of the bilateral relationship, in particular as it concerns security and defence cooperation. Franco-German defence cooperation is a symbol of Franco-German reconciliation and is built around a web of dense government-to-government and military-to-military relations, and defence-industrial links.[35] Elements include plans to develop a Main Ground Combat System (MGCS), an FCAS, a maritime-patrol aircraft, a joint C-130J unit that is to operate a total of ten transport and tanker aircraft (four French, six German) as a common fleet with shared airworthiness, maintenance and training facilities, and collaboration on a European medium-altitude long-endurance UAV.

When it comes to delivery, the track record of Franco-German collaboration is decidedly mixed. Defence-industrial policies and ownership structures as well as arms-export practice differ, operational experience and military requirements diverge, and regional priorities in security policy deviate. Thus, beyond the symbolism and political importance of Franco-German collaboration, the strategic outlook is very often less than compatible, which affects the viability of defence-industrial collaboration. While France thinks of its future main battle tank in terms of power projection and intervention, Germany is focused on the defence of NATO's eastern flank. Both views are reasonable given national threat perceptions and priorities, but they imply that France will put a greater emphasis on mobility, whereas Germany will likely emphasise firepower and protection. It is not possible to optimise all these parameters in one platform simultaneously. For France, the design drivers for a future combat aircraft include the requirement to be aircraft-carrier- and nuclear-capable, while Germany does not operate aircraft carriers and its nuclear role is much more limited than that of France. As a long-term connoisseur of Franco-German collaboration has suggested, Franco-German armaments cooperation is nearly an 'impossibility'.[36]

Arms-export policy is an area where Franco-German differences are evident and represent an indirect obstacle to successful defence-industrial and defence-procurement collaboration. The 2020 German defence-industrial strategy paper describes arms exports to EU and NATO members or countries with a NATO-equivalent status (Australia, Japan, New Zealand and Switzerland) as being in Germany's interest, primarily for three reasons.[37] Firstly, exports would lead to higher production runs, which would in turn bring down the price Germany would have to pay to purchase equipment it sources from its own industry. Secondly, larger order books would secure jobs, skills and technological capacity, and strengthen the competitiveness of the defence-industrial sector in Germany. Thirdly, if exports create equipment commonalities with countries that Germany might at some point operate alongside, that will yield interoperability benefits and make it easier to work together militarily. In contrast to France or the UK, however, Berlin does not acknowledge a fourth rationale: namely, it does not see arms exports as a foreign-policy instrument to gain leverage and influence. In practice, Germany's partners and industry perceive it as very restrictive in its export decisions.[38] Behind closed doors, officials from partner countries suggest that they consider it an advantage if a piece of military hardware is free of significant German components because it reduces the number of obstacles to export it. Some German industry representatives agree and have moved the production of certain items to sites outside Germany to gain more room for manoeuvre.[39] While Germany is at times accused of prioritising commercial interests over moral or strategic ones, as with the Nord Stream 2 pipeline, when it comes to exports that are directly lethal it is considered rather too scrupulous for its own good and that of its partners.

The preferences of the German government simultaneously to have a capable and sustainable defence-industrial base, closer European defence-industrial collaboration and restrictive arms exports are not compatible, creating an increasingly acute dilemma. In February 2019, then British foreign minister Jeremy Hunt wrote to German Foreign Minister Maas because of the German decision, announced in 2018, to freeze defence exports to Saudi Arabia over human-rights concerns, namely the Saudi-led intervention in Yemen and the killing of journalist Jamal Khashoggi. Hunt argued that such a freeze would create 'a real risk that Saudi Arabia may turn to Russian or Chinese supplies in future, depriving us of influence on Saudi International Humanitarian Law compliance' and that the decision would also have a negative impact 'on the supply chains of both UK and European defence industry'. He also suggested that 'the freeze on exports to Saudi Arabia will create a damaging lack of confidence in Germany's reliability as a partner and willingness to export jointly to third countries'.[40] France's ambassador in Berlin, Anne-Marie Descôtes, wrote in 2019 that German arms-export decisions are essentially unpredictable for France and suggested that Paris perceives that Berlin only considers the domestic political implications of those decisions, but not those for their partnerships.[41]

German arms-export policy thus creates significant tensions with other core German security-policy preferences, namely, to be a reliable partner in NATO and the EU and to pursue a stronger European dimension to security and defence with France. Germany's major NATO and EU partners, France and the UK, not only quite obviously see their arms-export relationships as bringing them political leverage over the purchaser, but they are also much more aggressive in supporting the commercial interests of their national defence-industrial bases.

Germany's choice to value human rights over arms exports in the case of Saudi Arabia might have been influenced by the fact that its defence industry is less exposed to exports to Riyadh than, for example, that of the UK, where a company like BAE Systems considers Saudi Arabia a key market in which it employs some 6,300 people, can expect to grow further and considers itself to be a part of the defence-industrial base.[42] Companies based in countries like the UK or France are increasingly likely to consider German involvement in their products as a risk to their supply chains and their route to markets. Partner governments will be equally irritated in particular if a consequence of a German export freeze is that their own access to equipment or weapons is also complicated because exports to different countries are run off the same licence, as occurred in the case of *Meteor* air-to-air missiles.[43] Since components made in Germany are part of many of the systems exported by other European nations, their national room for manoeuvre can rapidly evaporate if Germany exercises its power to block sales because of these components. French complaints include blocked exports to Saudi Arabia (on multiple occasions), Qatar, Uzbekistan, India and Niger.[44] In other cases, Germany was reportedly receptive to pressure and approved export decisions, including to Saudi Arabia after the 2018 freeze announcement, and thus occasionally vacates the moral high ground, making the approach overall somewhat inconsistent.[45]

While Germany consistently calls for the harmonisation of arms-export policies among EU member states to create a level playing field, France consistently stresses the importance of more flexible national approaches. France and Germany have several times tried to solve the issue of making export decisions on collaboratively developed and produced equipment and weapons. In the early 1970s, then defence ministers Helmut Schmidt and Michel Debré signed a joint letter that suggested they would not block each other from exporting and would not disrupt the supply chain unless exceptional circumstances applied. From the French perspective, Germany has increasingly moved away from this agreement. Another attempt was undertaken in form of an annex, finalised in October 2019, to the Treaty of Aachen, which does foresee a veto for export decisions if the export would negatively affect the national interests of either party, but also waives that veto power if the contribution to the overall product falls below a share agreed by the parties. However, what the German government refers to as 'war weapons' under the War Weapons Control Act – a list that includes munitions and projectiles, combat aircraft and helicopters, combat vehicles and naval vessels – are exempted from this so-called de minimis clause that would waive the right to veto. This elaborate compromise so far remains untested in practice.[46]

The wider background is that 25 years of cuts to defence spending, force structure and equipment holdings in Europe have increased the need for the defence industry to export to survive and generate returns. The defence industry today very much 'follows the money', and the money is increasingly outside home markets. If governments do not consider exports a desirable policy choice, then the other two options are either to consolidate and shrink industry and accept the job and skills losses this entails, as well as the dependencies on international suppliers, or to decide to finance a larger order book at home via large-scale defence-modernisation projects. France, Italy, Spain and the UK embrace the path of exporting internationally more or less enthusiastically, whereas Berlin does not. It seems implausible that France would develop with Germany future fighter aircraft, next-generation main battle tanks or artillery systems without the assumption that these will be made available for export so as to increase the economic viability of the projects and to use arms exports as a foreign-policy tool to gain influence with customer nations. At times the goal of developing and maintaining a capable defence industry to ensure that one's country is capable of self-defence may stand in tension with the goal of promoting liberal values and human rights abroad. Granting export licences and supporting international sales is neither automatically a wise choice nor automatically objectionable. Arms exports require a complex assessment: balancing the risks exports entail – including in terms of the stability of the recipient nation and the region more widely – with strategic interests, which might include alliances and partnerships, as well as economic motivations.

CHAPTER FOUR

A new strategic mindset

Berlin cannot continue its current tendency to make piecemeal, incremental revisions to existing security policy and punch below its weight in military terms if it hopes to adequately confront the fundamental shift in global order that is under way. The security repercussions of China's evolution into a peer competitor of the United States may be felt sooner in Europe than many anticipate. In March 2021, NATO Secretary-General Jens Stoltenberg argued that China's rise had 'direct consequences for our security', and US Secretary of State Antony Blinken suggested that 'there's no question that Beijing's course of behaviour threatens our collective security and prosperity … And that it is actively working to undercut the rules of the international system and the values we and our allies share.'[1] To confront this shift, Germany requires a new strategic mindset: one that assesses existing and potential threats to its security in a calm but clear-eyed manner and enables Berlin to respond by enacting the most effective security policy possible.

Working with natural allies
Powerful non-Western actors have made it clear, materially and ideologically, that they accept neither the power distribution

in the international order nor the value system characterising its institutional frameworks. Germany's goal should be to contribute effectively to the defence of Western values in the face of the incipient authoritarian challenge. The first step in doing so should be to relinquish any illusion that Berlin (and Europe more broadly) can navigate a comfortable middle path between the US and the authoritarian powers in the coming decades. Such a policy would be both morally and strategically deficient.

In ideological terms, the relative threat posed to Germany's liberal democracy by an emergent Chinese superpower and a revanchist Russia, compared to that posed by the US, is obvious. Notwithstanding a long history of transatlantic cultural and political differences, and justified European alarm at recent attempts to undermine democratic norms in the US, one of the poles in the evolving US–China rivalry remains the world's oldest continuous constitutional democracy, based on the principles (if not always the practice) of universal rights and the rule of law. The other is an increasingly ambitious authoritarian state governed by a party that between 1949 and 1976 killed tens of millions of its own citizens and which has recently established internment camps intended to suppress and brutalise an ethnic and religious minority.[2] Although Russia, unlike China, has no hope of rivalling the US in economic or military terms, it does have a policy of actively supporting and funding populist and extremist political movements within Europe.[3] Russian President Vladimir Putin and his confidants consider European liberal democracy and prosperity to be an ideological threat to their governing system, and therefore seek to undermine it.[4]

To an alarming extent, however, a significant proportion of Germans express a degree of ambivalence between the US and its authoritarian rivals, with some even considering that Washington poses a greater threat to Berlin than Moscow or Beijing does: in 2020, 25% (2019: 24%) of Germans felt that

China's foreign and security policy was a threat to German security; 30% (2019: 34%) said the same of Russia; and 37% (2019: 39%) thought so in relation to the US.[5] If Germans are concerned about defending the liberties they enjoy, they should not delude themselves that a reasonable policy would be to adopt strategic ambivalence between the forces that engendered and protected these liberties in Germany after 1945 and those forces that represent the antithesis of these liberties.

In strategic terms, those who imagine that Europe could or should form a third pole between Washington and Beijing fail to appreciate (or do not care) that China's best hope of overturning the current global supremacy of Western values and interests lies in any ability it may have to split the US from its European (and Asian) allies. Similarly, Russia is intent on pursuing a divide-and-rule policy, both between the US and European states, and within the European Union itself. Both Beijing and Moscow seek to employ tools including disinformation campaigns, cyber attacks, elite capture, economic pressure and investments in media infrastructure in Europe.[6] Chinese and Russian support for a multipolar world order is guided by their desire to diminish the role of the US. It is unsurprising therefore that some of the biggest supporters of the notion that Europe would serve as an alternative pole to the US live in Beijing and Moscow, although it would be more surprising if China or Russia sincerely hoped to see a Europe that was a strong and independent actor capable of asserting itself against them.

Among EU policymakers in Brussels and in some EU member-state capitals, the suggestion of a so-called 'Sinatra doctrine' in relation to the intensifying US–China rivalry has gained currency. In this context, Europe doing it 'My way' would imply a desire to decide for itself: avoiding automatic agreement with the US and on occasion cooperating with Beijing, while defending European interests and values against Chinese encroachment or even attack.[7] As Josep Borrell, high representative of the EU for foreign affairs and security policy and vice-president of the European Commission (and presumed author of the Sinatra doctrine), has argued, an independent view about two competitors does not equate to equidistance from them.[8] Borrell also suggested that, ultimately, such a doctrine would just be another way of saying 'strategic autonomy' or 'European sovereignty'. In this quest to carve out a space – in itself a reasonable and useful endeavour – some Europeans risk missing the plot: they should always wish to be strategic and enjoy the capability of acting autonomously if necessary, but not seek to assert independence simply for the sake of having a contrary position to the US. Put simply, if European decision-makers broadly share the US view on most issues regarding the security challenges emanating from China or Russia, they should come to the autonomous conclusion that it is in their strategic interest to work with the US. While the US and European states will never be perfectly aligned in their assessments of China or Russia, their chances of successfully defending the Western order will be significantly magnified if they can cooperate as effectively as possible against authoritarian encroachments. This basic equation would not be undermined but would be reinforced if European states were to develop the military capability to defend their own territory.

Practically speaking, in the coming years the EU will play a greater role in security cooperation between its member states as it seeks to implement a raft of initiatives ranging from the European Defence Fund (EDF) to Permanent Structured Cooperation (PESCO) to delivering better political–strategic guidance in the form of the so-called 'Strategic Compass' planned for 2022. The EU has gained in stature as a security-policy actor, and much of the current defence debate in Germany is informed by the assumption that a drive to further

European security cooperation is naturally the responsibility of the Franco-German partnership. However, NATO remains the most effective vehicle for Germany's military contribution to European defence and for transatlantic cooperation against Chinese and Russian threats. Unlike the EU, NATO includes both the US and the UK. The latter's military capabilities will form an essential component of any effort to ensure that Europe can defend itself. NATO allies benefit from existing command structures and more than 70 years of experience in cooperating, training and planning for major war.

NATO's credibility to deter and, if necessary, fight its adversaries has suffered both from the United States' recent underwhelming commitment under Donald Trump as well as from Germany's unreliability when it comes to its military spending and capability. NATO survived these challenges in part because it is an institutions-based alliance with formal structures that continue to function, even when strategic political cohesion is low. Alongside France and the UK, Germany now has an opportunity to provide leadership in a revitalised NATO, to work alongside its allies and through them serve as a net contributor to the security of Europe and the Western order more broadly. Germany could also play a constructive role in the effort to maintain unity within NATO as its members debate the extent to which its focus should be adapted to include direct security threats to Europe from China in addition to its traditional emphasis on Russia.

China

China's rapid economic growth in recent decades has afforded Germany many commercial opportunities. According to World Bank data, China is a notable export destination, the third largest for Germany after the US and France and ahead of the Netherlands, accounting for some 7% of German exports in 2018. It was also the largest importer to Germany ahead of the Netherlands and the US, accounting for just under 10% of German imports in 2018.[9] The political significance of this trade was visible in the remarks of certain CDU parliamentarians who in early 2021, while endorsing a 'strategically oriented transatlantic China policy', suggested at the same time that 'the means chosen should not infringe on the respective partner's economic well-being'.[10]

Beyond its short-term benefits from trade, in the longer term China's rise also threatens Germany's economic advantage and Western predominance more generally. The most significant metric in this context is not the proportion of economic exchange between China and Germany that might directly relate to security-relevant issues, but the insight that China's government is systematically connecting areas of economic, technological and military activity for the pursuit of its national strategic goals. It is the declared policy of the Chinese government to try to control future high-tech manufacturing, dominate areas of emerging technologies such as artificial intelligence (AI) and to become the global standard setter for next-generation technologies. This vision is established in the Made in China 2025 plan, the New Generation Artificial Intelligence Development Plan, and China Standards 2035.[11] It is a convenient myth, often repeated in German policy discussions, that China's political system is too rigid to enable innovation and technological breakthrough. Standard-setting provides the framework for future technology development, and technology development sets the conditions for future manufacturing. China is pursuing a strategy that seeks to redefine the rules of economic exchange and production on a global scale. New and emerging technologies will furthermore form an important part of its attempt to challenge the US militarily in the future. China is pursuing an overarching national strategy, supported and actively advanced by President Xi Jinping, of Military–Civil Fusion (MCF), once more attempting to align the levers of policy, economics, science and the armed forces to further its goals.

Beijing's economic vision is exploitative and predatory, grabbing what it can with little regard for the stability or well-being of others. China will continue to consider Germany, its second-largest destination of cumulative foreign direct investment in the EU between 2000 and 2019 (preceded only by the UK, which has since left the EU), as a source of technology.[12] Technology transfer takes multiple forms, ranging from China's acquisition of mature products that can be copied and manufactured in China for civilian and military use to its investment in blue-skies research and technology in order to acquire ideas rather than products. This has already been the case in Germany. In 2018, Ping An (China's largest insurer by market value) invested in Germany's fintech incubator Finleap GmbH through its 'Global Voyager Fund'.[13] That same year, Chinese tech giant Tencent invested in a Series C funding round for German online banking start-up N26. Tencent increased those investments in subsequent rounds in 2019 and 2020.[14] In 2019, Alibaba acquired Berlin-based start-up Data Artisans, a pioneer company in the stream processing of data, for US$103 million.[15] Real-time data-processing capability is crucial to developing the Internet of Things and AI applications. It would be unwise to believe that these technologies do not have military applications. Improving AI applications and analysing real-time data in the military realm could improve large-scale defence-mobilisation and targeting capabilities for autonomous systems.[16] The application of China's AI technologies is already evident in Beijing's approach to social control and large-scale surveillance networks across China.

It is certainly possible to overstate China's capabilities. Although its economy and military expenditure have grown rapidly – its official defence budget has grown in constant 2015 US$ terms from $99.3 billion in 2010 to $186bn in 2020[17] – it will face many internal political and economic challenges over the coming decades. It is instructive to recall the breathless predictions from the 1970s until the early 1990s that Japan would soon overtake the US economically. It is also important not to ignore enduring US and European strengths, notably their alliance networks. NATO is the most powerful political–military alliance in history; China's only formal military ally is North Korea. That said, in strategic terms China does have a certain advantage over European states: it is a more or less unitary actor and can attempt to play off European countries against each other and against the US. China would present a much less formidable challenge to international order if, as with European states, each of its provinces maintained independent security policies and armed forces.

It is difficult nowadays to find bipartisan agreement in Washington, but one comes closest with the near consensus that has emerged over the proposition that China's rise represents the primary threat to US interests over the coming decades. So far, US–China competition has been most overt in the economic realm, most notably with former US president Trump's 'trade war', but the parameters of a future military confrontation in East Asia are becoming increasingly clear. Xi has voiced the ambition for China to become the dominant military power in its region by 2035, and in the world by 2049.[18] Beijing has initiated an effort to transform the People's Liberation Army Navy (PLAN) and the PLA Air Force (PLAAF) into the dominant military forces in the Asia-Pacific littoral during 2020–35. Data tracked by the IISS for its Military Balance+ database illustrates the rapid pace of Chinese naval shipbuilding spanning everything from patrol crafts, corvettes and fleet support to amphibious assault ships, cruisers, destroyers and aircraft carriers. China's progress in advanced air-to-air weapons puts it in the vicinity of the most advanced Western systems; it has begun to field in operational service the J-20A, a fighter jet that challenges the previous US monopoly on operational stealth aircraft; and it doubled its heavy air-transport fleet between 2016 and 2020. The military effectiveness of the PLA as a fighting force remains limited by its lack of recent operational experience and shortcomings in training and doctrine. However, the intent is clear, the effort is systematic and it is showing results.

Within US policy circles, a growing alarm is manifesting that China is already approaching the point at which it could conceivably challenge US military superiority in East Asia and attempt an invasion of Taiwan, which it considers a renegade province. Prominent members of the US policy community have argued that Washington should reverse its policy of 'strategic ambiguity' and offer Taiwan an explicit security guarantee, in the hope that this would deter a Chinese attack.[19] In March 2021, Admiral Philip Davidson, commander of US Indo-Pacific Command, testified to Congress that China might try to invade Taiwan within the next six years.[20] In security terms, given the long time frames inherent in defence procurement and preparation, this threat is imminent – urgent, in fact.

On current trajectories, the US cannot be confident that it will be able to sustain its conventional military superiority in East Asia for much longer. Doing so would require a substantial effort and allocation of resources. Certainly, the US would not be able to fight a major conventional war with China in East Asia at the same time as another major conflict elsewhere, such as in Europe.[21] If major hostilities were to commence between China and the US, it is very likely that the US would reallocate to Asia assets that were normally committed to the European theatre. Europeans could most likely replace some of the US capabilities deployed in Europe, for example in the area of land forces and logistics. But strategic intelligence, surveillance and reconnaissance (ISR), large-scale command and control, air and missile defence including early warning, long-range bombers, large numbers of fifth-generation fighters and long-range precision-strike capabilities would all be in short supply. European states would find it very difficult or impossible to replace these capability shortfalls. The US government has designated the Indo-Pacific as a strategic priority and assigned a large number of forces to it. There should be no illusion that Europe would not be a lower-priority theatre, were the US forced to choose.

In 2020, Germany published a strategy for the Indo-Pacific, in recognition of this region's vital importance to its interests. However, this strategy notably included almost no reference to military issues, even though many existing or potential partners in the region remain deeply concerned about Chinese encroachments. While it is important to be realistic about the degree to which Germany or European allies can play a significant security role in the region, they could be of some assistance to the US and its Asian allies in their efforts to constrain Chinese military growth and assertiveness. For example, Germany could seek to play a leading role in establishing even stronger monitoring mechanisms for Chinese investments in sensitive European technologies – as well as starting to monitor at lower investment levels – or in efforts to systematically monitor and counter Chinese disinformation campaigns in a sustained way. European capabilities could also be used to provide security in the extended European periphery of the Mediterranean, Indian Ocean and Africa, where China seeks to establish influence. A still more direct action might be to participate in freedom-of-navigation operations in international waters that China claims as its own. In this context, it should be acknowledged that temporary deployments of naval vessels or a detachment of combat aircraft to Asia, both of which the German government is planning for 2021 and 2022, will have symbolic and political value, but would only be seen as a commitment to regional security by Germany's partners in the region if it led to persistent presence over a longer time period. Germany will also need to address the fundamental disjunction between its Indo-Pacific strategy document, which is explicitly intended to be inclusive and not directed against China, and the strategic outlook of its regional partners, who do perceive a direct threat from China and are preparing to defend against it. Given Europe's current difficulties in defending itself, it seems highly unlikely that German forces would ever participate in kinetic operations against China in the Indo-Pacific, no matter how bad US–China relations became. That said, the further development of German cyber or space capabilities could present Berlin with a formidable national asset, especially if those assets were sufficient to deter Chinese cyber interference in the European theatre that might occur in the context of Russian aggression.[22]

The most serious security implication for Germany of the US–China antagonism is, of course, an indirect one: because of the inevitable US military focus on East Asia, Germany will no longer be able to outsource its defence (and that of Europe more broadly) to the Americans. Germans take pride in the fact that their country exports large volumes of high-quality goods that are desired all around the world. But in security terms, Germany punches below its weight: it is a net security importer. China's rise means that Germany can no longer be a military liability and net security importer: it must be a net security exporter to Western and European defence.

The most immediate and constructive way for Berlin to do so would be to appreciate and address the real security threat that Russia poses to Europe. The probability that Putin, or another

Russian leader, would attempt to reconquer Eastern Europe, march to Berlin and reconstitute the Warsaw Pact is negligible, although some analysts have used this scenario's implausibility to argue that Europe can already credibly defend itself.[23] What is more likely is that Russia would exploit any security lacuna created by a US shift to Asia by using its considerable regional military power in a more limited fashion so as to undermine NATO and coerce European states.

Russia

Germany's future leaders, along with a significant proportion of the German people more generally, would be wise to acknowledge some basic realities about Russia. It has not democratised or reformed, and it is unlikely to do so for the foreseeable future. Although Russia suffers from myriad economic and political weaknesses and, unlike China, does not have the potential ability to shape a new world order, it is still strong enough to act as a 'spoiler' state within the existing order and on occasion exert coercive power.[24] In fact, its efforts to modernise its armed forces since the 2008 war with Georgia must count among the more successful Russian reform projects of the past 15 years. While it is worthwhile to be mindful of Russia's legitimate security concerns and avoid needless confrontation with it, this does not equate to adopting a wilful naivety about the worldview of Putin and those around him. Russia's leaders derive benefit from presenting European states and the US to the Russian populace as enemies, and their goal is for NATO and ultimately the EU to disintegrate.

Given the looming pressure on US military capabilities, Europeans will need to find an effective way to manage Russia themselves. In theory, this could be done through one of two approaches: rapprochement or more credible deterrence. At present, Europe's unofficial strategy towards China, driven by France since the G7 summit of August 2019 and tolerated by Germany, is based in part on the pursuit of rapprochement towards Moscow.[25] The goal has been to lure Russia away from China in order to isolate and weaken the latter. This approach has followed the classic precept of balance-of-power politics, according to which, if a systemic threat (i.e., China) arises to one's national interest, necessity suggests courting the weaker of two adversaries (i.e., Russia) to prevent closer alignment between them and draw the weaker one closer to one's own side.[26] In practice, though, for such an approach to be successful, the weaker of the two adversaries also needs to modify its hostile attitude. Crucially, the weaker adversary needs to want to agree to such a rapprochement and will most likely demand some form of compensation. As Putin is aware that his distancing from China would be designed to give the US and Europe a stronger hand regarding Beijing, his expected prize would likely be a costly one. Rather uncomfortably for Europeans, it is probable that the compensation for Russia's relinquishing its strategic flirtation with China is likely to come mainly at their expense. This could include a push for recognition of a Russian sphere of influence including Belarus and Ukraine; attempts to establish a veto on future EU and NATO enlargement, perhaps in the form of a new security treaty including Russia; a rollback of sanctions; and a revival of ideas for a modernisation partnership in which Europeans would be asked to pour money into Russia's dysfunctional and undiversified economy. It is not impossible that Germany and its European allies could one day reach some form of acceptable diplomatic agreement with Russia that lured it away from China, or at least persuaded it to adopt a neutral stance, without sacrificing the interests and democratic principles of other European states. Any deal, however, would need to be brokered from a position of European strength, not supplication. Germany and other European states would be more likely to obtain favourable terms from Russia – and minimise the risk of Moscow and Washington brokering a deal in which Europeans paid the primary price – if they developed military capabilities that are sufficient to defend their territory and deter Russian aggression even without active US involvement in that effort.

What kind of military threat does Russia pose to Germany and Europe, particularly within the context of Washington's increasing focus on East Asia? Russia's armed forces are obviously not on the scale that they were in the Soviet era. Yet following more than a decade of reforms, they have entered the 2020s better equipped, more professional, better trained and held at higher readiness than at any point since the end of the Cold War. Indeed, to move beyond Soviet-era mass mobilisation and establish a modern, high-readiness force has been the overriding success of the so-called 'New Look' reforms pursued since 2008. Russia's current military-modernisation process is optimised for short and decisive conventional military campaigns paired with a doctrine that allows for the application of its nuclear arsenal as a deterrent in an escalating confrontation.[27] It is easy to conceive how Russia might seek to use these forces to its advantage, if US military assets were essentially pinned down in East Asia by a mounting confrontation or actual conflict with China.

At present, were the European members of NATO (which we refer to as NATO-Europe) solely responsible for European defence and unable to draw on US capabilities, it is likely that they would struggle to respond militarily to a scenario in which Russia undertook a limited land grab of some NATO territory (for example in the Baltic states), started negotiating for a ceasefire while also making frequent references to its nuclear capability. The IISS explored such a scenario in some depth in 2019 and concluded that NATO-Europe would have capability gaps that would cost between US$290bn and US$360bn to address and would take about 15 years to do so. Notable capability gaps include air and missile defence, advanced fighter aircraft and the need to recapitalise large parts of the European armoured-vehicle fleets.[28]

This scenario of a limited conventional war is a hard one for NATO-Europe because it plays to Russian strengths and exploits European weaknesses. It assumes that the Russian objective is to destroy NATO, not to occupy large swathes of Central or Western Europe. By violating NATO territory, Russia would pose a twofold challenge: if the provocation went unanswered because NATO-Europe could not muster the cohesion to fight, it is likely that NATO would be finished, at least in the long run. A military alliance that does not adequately respond to aggression has lost its value. If NATO-Europe did fight, it would need to fight an offensive campaign to retake the territory Russia had occupied. To do so successfully, it would need to achieve superior force ratios in relation to what would likely be deployed on the Russian side. This would make the task far from simple, especially in the face of significant Russian long-range-strike capability that puts the territory of all European NATO members at risk; sophisticated and layered Russian air defence that would be costly to degrade; and the spectre of nuclear escalation. Essentially the deterrence task for NATO-Europe vis-à-vis Russia is to generate enough conventional military capability so that a short war would be unwinnable for Moscow.[29]

In recent years, there has been significant speculation and debate about the extent to which a security axis may be emerging between Moscow and China, whether formal or informal.[30] Russia would be the junior partner in such a configuration but would probably perceive enough complementarity with China to make it worthwhile.[31] While formal political–military cooperation between Moscow and Beijing would indeed present a formidable challenge for Western states, this would not be necessary for our analysis to hold. NATO-Europe would face a daunting challenge responding to any Russian opportunistic attempt to undermine the Alliance while the US was preoccupied by a US–China confrontation in Asia, even if Putin had not coordinated his adventure with Beijing or concluded a security pact.

In addition to an 'acute' scenario in which Putin might seek to break NATO through a political–military gambit in Eastern Europe, Germany should also consider the threat of 'chronic' Russian pressure, in which a Europe fundamentally unwilling to protect itself effectively against Russia became vulnerable to long-term Russian coercion and potentially a process of 'Finlandisation' in Eastern Europe, undermining the autonomy of European states. Considering Russia's current behaviour, while US forces remain in Europe, it would be rash to assume that Putin (or a more aggressive successor) would behave in a more amenable fashion once US conventional forces were essentially devoted to the Indo-Pacific and before Germany and its allies had established a credible deterrent against Russian incursions.

Germany's strategic goal should be to ensure that NATO-Europe is capable of deterring Russia and ultimately defending itself in a Russian land-grab scenario. This would require a significant reconceptualisation of German security policy, defence expenditure and use of military force. Germany would need to acknowledge that, to deter Russia, it would need both the will and the capability to lead any projection of military power at scale and at speed eastwards for the purpose of defending Europe in a high-intensity, war-fighting scenario. It would also require a serious debate about the role of nuclear deterrence in German defence.

Thinking clearly about nuclear deterrence

NATO-Europe includes two nuclear powers: France and the UK. France's nuclear deterrent comprises a naval component based on four *Triomphant*-class nuclear-powered ballistic-missile submarines (SSBNs) operating a continuous at-sea deterrent, and an air-force component based on *Rafale* aircraft equipped with ASMPA cruise missiles. A naval-aviation component can be added by presidential request, based on *Rafale* aircraft deployed to the carrier *Charles de Gaulle*. Command authority rests with the French president. The UK's nuclear deterrent is based on its four *Vanguard*-class SSBNs, which operate a continuous at-sea deterrent. Design work has begun on the successor to the *Vanguard*, to be known as the *Dreadnought* class. The first-of-class is anticipated to enter service in the early 2030s. The UK is participating in the United States' *Trident* life-extension programme, which is intended to keep the missile in service into the early 2040s. Command authority for the launch of nuclear weapons rests with the British prime minister.

In addition, under the dual-capable aircraft (DCA) element of NATO's deterrence posture, a number of US-owned free-fall nuclear bombs are stored in Belgium, Germany, Italy, the Netherlands and Turkey. The air forces of these countries have the capacity to carry and deliver those weapons, but the US retains control and custody of them.[32] The purpose of the forward-deployed US weapons is to strengthen the credibility of extended deterrence – the ability of US nuclear weapons to deter an attack on its European NATO allies. The credibility of such extended deterrence, which would entail the willingness of a US president to risk, say, the destruction of a major US city in order to prevent a European one from being captured, has been contested for decades.[33] In addition, Trump's presidency, which was marked by several moments in which the president directly undermined Washington's commitment to NATO's defence, has made reliance on the US strategic nuclear deterrent less plausible for many Europeans.

Russia continues to modernise its strategic nuclear weapons – a capability area that received investment even before the current Russian defence-reform process began – while also improving its theatre nuclear weapons. China's nuclear forces are primarily land based but it is developing a naval capability, while the air force is expected to regain a nuclear mission with the entry into service of a new bomber design in the second half of the 2020s. It could do so earlier pending the introduction of dual-capable aero-ballistic missiles on a variant of the H-6 bomber. China's ballistic-missile arsenal is undergoing modernisation, with updated versions of existing designs, and new types, such as the DF-41 (CH-SS-X-20) intercontinental-range missile, currently in various stages of development and deployment. On balance, the nuclear-modernisation processes of potential adversaries, the doctrinal development of adversaries and the US focus on Asia, with its explicit consequence that Europe is not the priority theatre for the US, again raise concerns about the credibility of the existing nuclear posture in NATO. The UK, for example, announced in 2021 the decision to raise the ceiling on its stockpile of nuclear warheads after a long period of reductions, a sign of concerns within the British government about the credibility of the country's deterrence posture given changes in the nuclear capabilities and postures of possible adversaries.

Germany needs to think seriously about the credibility of its own contribution to the European pillar of NATO's nuclear deterrence. Essentially, its options are threefold. Firstly, Germany could withdraw from the NATO DCA arrangement or simply not renew its capacity to participate in it. This would not change the fact that NATO as an alliance will continue to rely on nuclear weapons as part of its deterrence –

with conventional forces and missile defence being the other key components. This pathway would only serve to deprive Germany of significant influence over NATO's nuclear policy and strategy.

Secondly, Germany could go in the opposite direction and develop its own nuclear weapons. This would carry a political and diplomatic price that would be unsustainable for Berlin. Indeed, German Minister of Defence Annegret Kramp-Karrenbauer, in a speech in October 2020, insisted that 'we cannot provide our own nuclear deterrence, nor do we want to. This is why America must remain by our side and protect us.'[34] This points to the third option available to Germany, namely to continue to benefit from its allies' nuclear deterrents. However, Kramp-Karrenbauer did not explain how Germany could contribute to making that allied nuclear deterrent effective and credible. In fact, in conceptual terms, her remarks were reminiscent of an earlier era in which European NATO members were engaged in what Michael Howard described as a 'process whereby European Governments ... sought greater security by demanding an ever greater intensification of the American nuclear commitment'.[35] Given its political sensitivity, German decision-makers should begin thinking now about the ways in which Berlin and other European states could play a stronger role in NATO's nuclear-deterrence posture.

CHAPTER FIVE

Elements of a new security policy

Angela Merkel will most likely go down in history as a remark-
able chancellor who successfully steered Germany through
challenging times with thoughtfulness and determination. At
the end of her fourth term, she, personally, remains popular
with voters – a fact that itself captures her qualities as a political
leader. Yet Merkel's successor will inherit German underperformance in security and defence policy. Her policies did not
create this underperformance, but they failed to remedy it. For
the most part, Germany's political leadership does not possess
a strategic mindset – the understanding that power politics and
military force are unavoidable features of international politics
– and has therefore failed to translate the nation's considerable
resources into an effective security policy. As the journalist
Lorenz Hemicker put it, Germans think of the Bundeswehr like
home-contents insurance: it is good to know that it is there, it
should not cost much, and if it is ever needed it should cover
everything.[1] This is a comforting illusion, but such criteria
are impossible to fulfil in the realm of national defence. The
Bundeswehr is underfunded, ill equipped and enjoys poor
value for money with its procurements. Despite its professed

intentions, Germany is not a reliable partner for its allies in the security realm. Indeed, the ongoing assumption among many in Berlin, whether spoken or unspoken, is that Germany must continue to rely on others for its own defence. Germany is therefore also not equipped to defend an international order whose essential elements are contested and undermined by powerful actors hostile to Western norms, nor is it well positioned to contribute substantially to the evolution of that order to make sure it is fit for the coming decades.

There are many reasons why Germany lacks the strategic mindset that should inform its security policy.[1] The most obvious is its particularly bloody history of militarism and conquest, from which many Germans have inferred a national responsibility never again to use military force outside Germany itself. This worldview was most understandable in the decades immediately after 1945; indeed, it was effectively demanded by West Germany's neighbours, and Bonn's contribution to collective security was in practice essentially the defence of its own territory. In the late 1990s and early 2000s, Germany faced additional external pressure to adapt its security policy, but the security challenges were less direct in nature. Now, however, the international order upon which German security and prosperity

---

I   There is a parallel between Germany's current reluctance to include the use of lethal military force as part of its statecraft and its reluctance to engage in what most of its partner states (and certainly its adversaries) would consider the routine business of secret intelligence: stealing the secrets of others. In the realm of intelligence, Germany tends to adopt an overly legalistic approach and insist upon levels of scrutiny and transparency that are unacceptable for many of its partners, complicating international intelligence cooperation. It has favoured a strong analytical rather than operational culture and, in line with broader policies, sought to be active in multilateral fora where the emphasis is on analysis rather than outcomes. A further parallel is the tendency of German politicians to keep the intelligence agencies at arm's length and not take ownership of their activities. While this book does not consider intelligence or intelligence reform in detail, it seems likely that any security policy imbued with a strategic mindset would need to adopt a similarly realistic approach to the use of secret intelligence as it would to the use of military force.

depend is under threat. The finite military resources of the United States means that its conventional forces will be unable to counter the armed forces of both China and Russia. The rise of China therefore presents an indirect but imminent threat to Europe's security, one that decision-makers in Berlin have inadequately internalised. For Europe to deter Russia and defend itself without US conventional capabilities and an overreliance on the US strategic nuclear deterrent that may appear increasingly less credible, Germany will need not only to start pulling its weight in security terms, but also to adopt a leadership role commensurate with its economic and demographic stature. Germany must consider how it can become a net exporter, rather than a net importer, of 'hard' security, and how this security can not only serve humanitarian purposes but also protect the interests of Germany and its allies. This is not a matter for gradual evolution or adaptation: although the threat to NATO's eastern flank may be several years away, in defence terms it is already on Germany's doorstep. The time remaining for Germany's democratic leaders to change their outlook significantly – and mobilise sufficient political support to make the necessary changes to national security policy – is short.

Were Germany to adopt a strategic mindset, as we have argued it should, it is useful to consider how this might manifest in a new security policy that sought to remedy some of the shortfalls we have identified. The purpose of such an exercise is to think, within reasonable parameters, about possible practical implications of our argument. It is not to offer a counsel of perfection or an ideal and unrealistic policy 'wish list' that, if followed, would supposedly guarantee national success. We have no desire to provide a false sense of certainty or, as one finds in many think-tank reports, a list of bullet-point policy recommendations that purport to resolve neatly the profound challenges that have been identified. But it is helpful to consider what a revitalised, 'strategic' security policy could look like, if only to stimulate imagination and offer food for thought to those Germans willing to think seriously about their country's next steps.

While it would be useful to give some tangible form to the process of adopting a strategic mindset, and policy choices will eventually need to be codified to have a lasting impact, our primary concern is not to argue for a new strategy document, whatever its name or precise scope. Such a document would help institutionalise, and thus make more durable, the views, arguments and options informing German leaders, the electorate and international partners, but it would be a result of, rather than a precondition or even catalyst of, Germany's adopting a strategic mindset.

Any efforts to rethink Germany's security policy would benefit from an effort to integrate the perspectives of Germany's major international partners in the EU and NATO, but also of those nations in the Indo-Pacific that Berlin has identified as key regional partners, such as Australia, Japan, Singapore and South Korea. Doing so will help Berlin – as it would any other capital – to avoid a purely introspective reflection, provide useful external challenges to entrenched assumptions and serve as an opportunity to strengthen consensus among partners.

As we have argued, Germany's strategic goal should be to contribute to the defence of the Western international order against the assertive, expansionist and authoritarian regimes of China and Russia in a way commensurate with its political and economic stature. Germany has a responsibility to do so because it was that same order that enabled its own rehabilitation in the form of a liberal and prosperous democracy after the militaristic excesses of its past. It is in its interest to do so because that order continues to underpin the liberty and prosperity of Germany and its allies. The instruments it can employ to achieve this strategic goal should be drawn from the full spectrum of foreign policy and national power, including military power. It is in the latter category that Germany has underperformed dramatically, and where the gap between what Germany could do as a leading member of the Euro-Atlantic community and what it chooses to do is most pronounced; hence it is the focus of our analysis. In terms of defence policy, the strategic goal translates into important capability ambitions that are a far cry from the static defence of territory that would have been the Bundeswehr's focus at the end of the Cold War: to generate the military capability to establish Germany as the leading European land power able to defend NATO's eastern flank; to maintain the ability to conduct military crisis-management operations in Europe's periphery, and to provide a power-projection capability via air and naval assets to establish a persistent presence in the Indo-Pacific in order to signal intent and an enduring commitment to regional security there; and to invest in cyber and space-based capabilities to defend against hybrid attacks designed to undermine the resilience and cohesion of NATO and EU member states.

If Germany had those capabilities, it would considerably strengthen the European pillar of NATO, contribute to better burden-sharing in the Alliance and lessen the load the US carries as it seeks to balance its global security obligations. To its European partners – in NATO and the EU – Berlin would be sending a reassuring signal that it will accept a sizeable burden in order to make multilateral cooperation for the defence of Europe effective. To those countries that Germany has recently identified as strategic partners in the Indo-Pacific, Berlin would offer recognition that their security concerns and those of Europe are connected and form a shared agenda. From that position, Germany would be able to contribute to the defence of the international order from which it benefits but also the evolution of that order, to ensure it reflects future needs.

The list of practical issues that would need to be tackled to make progress on this strategic agenda over the coming decade is long but would begin with communication. Germany's strategic culture, or rather the societal preferences that it entails, has traditionally set limits on what foreign- and security-policy behaviour would be deemed acceptable. But public opinion has begun to shift due to a sense of uncertainty and genuine concerns about developments in global politics. Senior leaders will need to both respond to these concerns and show leadership in transforming public opinion in order to build a new domestic consensus. The fact that democratic leaders require electoral approval does not preclude policy-makers from leading public opinion rather than being led by it. We are not arguing that threats, risks or challenges should be amplified unnecessarily to influence public opinion. But we are suggesting that, so far, there has not been a systematic, clear and level-headed communication to the German people of the fact that powerful external actors do not seek compromise with or integration into the Western order, but in fact seek to undermine the foundations of Germany's current security, prosperity and way of life. It is unwise to downplay the potential consequences of a successful contestation of the existing world order by powers with very different ideas of individual liberties, social control, the rule of law, and political and economic exchange between nations. The public does not need to be shielded from what Sir Lawrence Freedman has described as the 'dark side to the strategic imagination that picks up intimations of disorder at times of stability, that senses the fragility of human institutions even while striving to reinforce them, that cannot stop thinking of war while promoting peace'.[2] In terms of democratic communication, the challenge lies in avoiding abstract notions of strategic problems that on the surface seem to have little to do with the everyday lives of the electorate while at the same time capturing the magnitude and importance of the problem.

The second core issue to tackle is money. There was a time when Germany managed to maintain significant levels of defence spending and generous social spending simultaneously. In 1990, public social spending in Germany stood at over 21% of GDP and defence spending at approximately 2.4% of GDP.[3] A healthy welfare state and healthy armed forces are not mutually exclusive. In 2020, even accounting for the downturn inflicted by the COVID-19 pandemic, Germany's GDP stood at €3.332 trillion.[4] Defence spending at the 2.4% of GDP allocated in 1990 would have amounted to a defence budget of some €80 billion, compared to the €44.9bn that Germany did spend. Even spending at the agreed 2014 NATO guideline of 2% of GDP would have amounted to about €67bn. But a particular percentage of GDP is an arbitrary metric when it comes to strategic questions. The real question is: how much is enough?

IISS analysis conducted in 2019 estimated that the capability gaps that NATO-Europe currently faces in relation to a state-on-state conventional war would require an initial investment by European NATO member states of about US$350bn.[5] The analysis envisioned that this additional money would be expended over the course of at least ten years. The expenditure would be devoted primarily to equipment procurement. We assume that procurement costs represent about 20% of the total life-cycle cost of equipment and the other 80% is soaked up by operations and support during the in-service period, which can last decades.[6] For the sake of argument, we can assume that one-third of the full life-cycle costs would need to be budgeted for the coming decade (a very generous assumption used to establish the upper boundary, given that operations and support costs peak at a much later state of active use). This would equate to a total financial commitment from all European NATO member states of about US$465bn for operations and support (assuming total life-cycle cost of four times the cost of acquisition). Germany currently aims to provide 10% of capability in the NATO context. For NATO-Europe, we could assume that would translate to 30%. Total acquisition cost plus operations and service would amount to US$810bn over a decade; if Germany were to assume 30% of that burden, it would amount to US$243bn (about €202bn) over ten years. In other words, even using the upper-boundary estimate (giving the maximum obligation for Germany) and front-loading the spending cycle, the required additional spending would still be encompassed within the 2%-of-GDP NATO goal. It is safe to assume that this additional spending would also enable the Bundeswehr to do on a regular basis what it has started to do on an ad hoc basis in 2021: namely, to enable a military presence in Asia. It would also strengthen Germany's ability to provide crisis-management capacity in the wider European neighbourhood. It would be helpful to establish a legal framework that would allow the Ministry of Defence to work with a multi-year budget framework, like the French military-programming law. This would represent a substantial shift and would require strong political leadership from the very top of German governments. Politicians would need to make the argument to the electorate that this expenditure is not just possible – which it is – but also necessary.

For additional defence spending to have a meaningful effect by generating extra capability and improving readiness – including through larger and more frequent exercises and a stronger focus on maintenance, repair and overhaul of equipment – Germany's procurement and acquisition process must improve. For several years, efforts in this area have focused on addressing staffing shortfalls in departments that deal with procurement, enhancing the rigour of contracts, introducing risk-management techniques and streamlining overly complex bureaucratic processes. The measures are designed to optimise the processes and procedures of procurement and acquisition to achieve better value for money and faster implementation while ensuring that programmes remain focused on the Bundeswehr's requirements. These efforts have led to improvements in some areas but have not delivered a breakthrough.[7] This is unlikely to change if the reform of procurement and acquisition continues to be guided by a mindset of process optimisation but suffers from a 'strategy deficit'.[8] The current reform goals are not incorrect, but they are likely to produce marginal results, as better processes in a strategic vacuum are insufficient. The strategic goals we suggest can serve to develop the overarching guidance: for what purpose and role should the Bundeswehr be equipped? This question can direct the application of better processes but also inform possible ideas such as modular and interoperable equipment, buying off-the-shelf where possible, avoiding overspecification of requirements, and international collaboration on procurement.

Technology is not a panacea for the armed forces or for German security policy more generally. By itself, it does not even necessarily imply a gain in military capability. Unless technology is embedded deeply in doctrine, operational concepts, training and education, its introduction may well erect hurdles for the successful application of military force and create new vulnerabilities.[9] Germany has responded late to attempts by others to harness emerging technologies for defence purposes and the debate remains strongly influenced by the desire to regulate and to control. It is appropriate to define ethical and legal boundaries to the exploitation of technology but there should be no illusion that all parties to future armed conflict will apply those rules. Therefore, it is necessary to strengthen the argument for innovation as a tool that can generate military advantage – not just commercial advantage – for Germany and its partners.

As we have argued, Germany should continue to benefit from the nuclear deterrence provided by its allies and contribute to nuclear-sharing arrangements like the NATO dual-capable aircraft (DCA) arrangement. Planning for a stronger European deterrent is an undertaking that will be politically extremely sensitive. It would need to begin with discussions with the UK and France. If a European deterrent were founded on even a small number of stand-off weapons, it is plausible that the number of warheads required would be less than what is commonly assumed to be committed in NATO at present, including via the DCA arrangement, since stand-off systems make deterrence more credible than the current free-fall bombs. The reason is simple: a free-fall bomb essentially needs to be delivered by an aircraft and dropped over the target. Even advanced fighter jets would struggle to penetrate layered air defence of the kind that, for example, Russia possesses. Given that a large proportion of aircraft would be lost in the attempt to deliver free-fall bombs, more aircraft and more weapons would be needed to ensure that some breached the defences and delivered their load. Air- and submarine-launched cruise missiles could be fired from beyond the opponent's air-defence zone and thus mitigate this challenge. Current DCA arrangements, although based on US weapons, provide clues on how to involve allies in nuclear tasks while managing proliferation concerns and could therefore be a starting point for discussions between Berlin, Paris and London. As François Heisbourg has argued, Paris might be open to such a conversation but that will not be a sufficient condition for success unless Germany pursues it with some determination as well. He foresees, for example, a rotational presence of French dual-capable aircraft outside French territory. In addition, it might be advisable to discuss making a small number of French ASMPA supersonic cruise missiles available to Germany in extreme circumstances and under procedures guided by DCA-type arrangements.[10]

To begin moving German security and defence policy in the direction we have suggested will require a significant degree of political leadership, along with substantial and substantive discussions in national-security bodies and parliament, informed and assisted by expertise from academia and think tanks. The frequent lament from the 1990s and early 2000s that there was no debate about security policy among the policy community in Berlin is no longer accurate. But that debate is limited in depth and narrow in scope. Far from being a marketplace of ideas, it is perhaps better described as an echo chamber for established views on multilateralism, arms control and international institutions. Germany, unlike many of its partners, does not have a national-security strategy, nor a national-security decision-making apparatus designed to facilitate the coordination and integration of the views of different stakeholders in government that would be desirable considering the current complexity and the multitude of challenges. The security and defence discourse in parliament often focuses on questions of individual procurement decisions or specific Bundeswehr missions but rarely on the fundamental underlying strategic issues. The number of experts in the German analytical community that would self-identify as strategic-studies scholars is very small.

For a new strategic mindset to develop, the executive and legislative branches of German government – and those who advise them – need new perspectives and venues in which to debate them. The debate about whether Germany needs a document that is explicitly styled as a national-security strategy and a national-security council that actively coordinates policy processes across agencies and ministries is now well into its second decade.[11] What is known, not least from the experiences of Germany's partners, is that inter-ministerial and interagency structures do play an important role in the implementation of strategy. Given the complexity of the international challenges confronting Germany and its partners and the rapid pace of international change, however, such structures would need to do more than simply coordinate perspectives – they would need to *integrate* the perspectives of the different stakeholders to prioritise policy objectives, drive their implementation and ensure the coherence of German security policy over time and issue areas. In contrast to many of its core partners, Germany currently does not have an institutional structure to achieve this. To be effective, any such structure or body would need to be invested with the authority of the chancellor.

We have argued that Germans should adopt a healthier and more constructive understanding of their historical inheritance. This is not the responsibility to subscribe to an immoral and irresponsible pacifism, but the responsibility to use German power for good; namely, to defend the liberal-democratic values of the Western order, and to defend that order itself from its enemies. An acknowledgement of this 'responsibility to defend' would recognise both that Germany's previous actions can never be forgotten, and that those actions do not absolve Germans today of their duty to contribute to the protection of the order and the alliance that have safeguarded their liberty and prosperity for much of the past century, and whose successful defence will remain indispensable to the preservation of German interests.

We do not pretend this will be an easy task. The next German chancellor will face an array of domestic and foreign challenges clamouring for their attention. At the same time, they will face significant opposition to any concerted attempt to lead a broader societal reconceptualisation of the role of military power within German statecraft. Easy or not, this task will be unavoidable if Germany is to meet the challenges it faces over the next decade. Communicating those challenges clearly to the electorate, and devising policy to meet them, is a task for political leadership.

NOTES

Introduction

1   Karl Vick and Simon Shuster, 'Chancellor of the Free World', *Time*, December 2015, http://time.com/time-person-of-the-year-2015-angela merkel/?iid=coverrecirc; 'The Indispensable European', *The Economist*, 7 November 2015, http://www.economist.com/news/leaders/21677643-angela-merkel-facesher-most-serious-political-challengeyet-europe-needs-her-more; and 'Germany Is Doomed to Lead Europe', *The Economist*, 25 June 2020, https://www.economist.com/europe/2020/06/25/germany-is-doomed-to-lead-europe.

2   For more on this issue, see Markus Kaim and Constanze Stelzenmüller, *New Power, New Responsibility: Elements of a German Foreign and Security Policy for a Changing World* (Berlin: Stiftung Wissenschaft und Politik and Washington DC: German Marshall Fund of the United States, 2013), especially pp. 12–17.

3   Ralf Neukirch, 'Deutschlands Neue Außenpolitik: Westerwelles Widersinnige Doktrin' [Germany's New Foreign Policy: Westerwelle's Absurd Doctrine], *Der Spiegel*, 29 March 2011, https://www.spiegel.de/politik/deutschland/deutschlands-neue-aussenpolitik-westerwelles-widersinnige-doktrin-a-753759.html.

4   Xuewu Gu, 'Der Dritte Weg: Warum Europa den Alleingang Wagen Muss' [The Third Way: Why Europe Must Dare to Go It Alone], *Handelsblatt*, 22 November 2019, https://www.handelsblatt.com/meinung/gastbeitraege/gast-kommentar-der-dritte-weg-warum-europa-den-alleingang-wagen-muss/25253468.html?ticket=ST-9936575-B4D3QfoN3kpM2QxpSUGM-ap5.

5   Stuart Lau and Laurenz Gehrke, 'Merkel Sides With Xi on Avoiding Cold War Blocs', Politico, 26 January 2021, https://www.politico.eu/article/merkel-sides-with-xi-on-avoiding-cold-war-blocs/#.

6   Hung Tran, 'Xi Jinping at the Virtual Davos: Multilateralism With Chinese Characteristics', New Atlanti-

cist blog, Atlantic Council, 26 January 2021, https://www.atlanticcouncil.org/blogs/new-atlanticist/xi-jinping-at-the-virtual-davos-multilateralism-with-chinese-characteristics/.

7   Constanze Stelzenmüller, 'Germany Is Pouring Cold Water on the Biden–Europe Love Fest', *Foreign Policy*, 22 January 2021, https://foreignpolicy.com/2021/01/22/germany-biden-europe-love-fest/.

8   'Peter Altmaier Hält Sanktionen Gegen Russland für Wenig Wirksam' [Peter Altmaier Considers Sanctions Against Russia to Be Ineffective], Zeit Online, 8 September 2020, https://www.zeit.de/politik/deutschland/2020-09/giftanschlag-alexej-nawalny-russland-sanktionen-peter-altmaier.

9   Die Bundesregierung [Cabinet of Germany], 'Leitlinien zum Indo-Pazifik' [Policy Guidlines for the Indo-Pacific], 1 September 2020, https://www.auswaertiges-amt.de/blob/2380500/33f978a9d4f511942c241eb4602086c1/200901-indo-pazifik-leitlinien--1--data.pdf.

10 Johannes Leithäuser, 'Deutschland Entsendet Fregatte in Ostasiatische Gewässer' [Germany Sends Frigates to East Asian Waters], *Frankfurter Allgemeine Zeitung*, 2 March 2021, https://www.faz.net/aktuell/politik/inland/deutschland-entsendet-fregatte-in-indo-pazifik-raum-17224589.html#void.

11 European Commission and HR/VP contribution to the European Council, 'EU–China – A Strategic Outlook', 12 March 2019, p. 1, https://ec.europa.eu/info/sites/info/files/communication-eu-china-a-strategic-outlook.pdf.

12 Frank-Walter Steinmeier, 'Rede von Außenminister Frank-Walter Steinmeier Anlässlich der 50. Münchner Sicherheitskonferenz' [Speech by Foreign Minister Frank-Walter Steinmeier at the 50th Munich Security Conference], 1 February 2014, https://www.auswaertiges-amt.de/en/newsroom/news/140201-bm-muesiko/259556.

13 David E. Sanger and Steven Erlanger, '"The West Is Winning," Pompeo Said. The West Wasn't Buying It', *New York Times*, 15 February 2020, https://www.nytimes.com/2020/02/15/world/europe/pompeo-munich-conference.html; and '"Wir Koennen Uns Nicht Wegducken": Schäuble Fordert Stärkeres Militärisches Engagement Deutschlands' ['We Can't Duck Away': Schäuble Calls for Germany to Be More Involved Militarily], *Der Tagesspiegel*, 31 January 2020, https://www.tagesspiegel.de/politik/wir-koennen-uns-nicht-wegducken-schaeuble-fordert-staerkeres-militaerisches-engagement-deutschlands/25494404.html.

14 Christoph von Marschall, '"Heraushalten Ist Keine Option": Schäuble Fordert Stärkeres Militärisches Engagement Deutschlands' ['Staying Out Is Not an Option': Schäuble Calls for Germany to Be More Involved Militarily], *Der Tagesspiegel*, 29 October 2019, https://www.tagesspiegel.de/politik/heraushalten-ist-keine-option-schaeuble-fordert-staerkeres-militaerisches-engagement-deutschlands/25166690.html.

15 Heiko Biehl, Bastian Giegerich and Alexandra Jonas, 'Introduction', in Heiko Biehl, Bastian Giegerich and Alexandra Jonas (eds), *Strategic Cultures in Europe: Security and Defence Policies Across the Continent* (Wiesbaden: Springer VS, 2013), pp. 7–17. Of course, judgements about a national strategic culture are to a certain extent subjective. Our judgements about German strategic culture

derive from our combined decades of observation and participation in Germany's strategic discourse.

16 Quentin Skinner, *Machiavelli* (Oxford: Oxford University Press, 1981), p. 31. See also John Greville Agard Pocock, *The Machiavellian Moment: Florentine Political Thought and the Atlantic Republican Tradition* (Princeton, NJ: Princeton University Press, 1975). Raymond Aron explained how the enduring value of Machiavelli's 'revolution' is that interest in his work 'always thrives when order is challenged … [It is] a rise in consciousness coinciding with a period in which order … becomes the issue at stake', in Raymond Aron, *Politics and History* (Piscataway, NJ: Transaction Publishers, 1983), p. 244.

17 Skinner, *Machiavelli*, chapter 18. While not referencing Machiavelli, Hans-Peter Schwarz had already made a similar suggestion in 1985, in Hans-Peter Schwarz, *Die Gezähmten Deutschen: Von der Machtbesessenheit zur Machtvergessenheit* [The Tamed Germans: From Power Obsession to Power Amnesia] (Stuttgart: Deutsche Verlags-Anstalt, 1985), p. 165.

18 See, for example, Joshua Posaner and Nette Nöstlinger, 'Merkel to Biden: Europe Ready to "Take on More Responsibility"', Politico, 9 November 2020, https://www.politico.eu/article/angela-merkel-joe-biden-europe-will-take-more-responsibility/.

19 Biden has explicitly called on European allies to cooperate against the threat from China. See, for example, White House, 'Remarks by President Biden at the 2021 Virtual Munich Security Conference', 19 February 2021, https://www.whitehouse.gov/briefing-room/speeches-remarks/2021/02/19/ remarks-by-president-biden-at-the-2021-virtual-munich-security-conference/; and Demetri Sevastopulo, 'US vs China: Biden Bets on Alliances to Push Back Against Beijing', *Financial Times*, 4 March 2021, https://www.ft.com/content/cf71feb2-297f-4e3a-8627-b89931cc6a80.

20 See Martin Jäger, 'Neue Strategische Lage: Deutschland Sollte Interventionsfähig Sein' [New Strategic Situation: Germany Should Be Able to Intervene], *Frankfurter Allgemeine Zeitung*, 6 September 2020, https://www.faz.net/aktuell/politik/inland/deutschland-sollte-interventionsfaehig-sein-neue-strategische-lage-16938806.html; and Wolfgang Schäuble, '"Globale Verantwortung als nationale Herausforderung": Rede beim Festakt zur Verabschiedung von Volker Perthes als Direktor der Stiftung Wissenschaft und Politik' ['Global Responsibility as a National Challenge': Speech at the Farewell Ceremony of Volker Perthes as Director of the German Institute for International and Security Affairs], 9 September 2020, https://www.swp-berlin.org/fileadmin/contents/products/sonstiges/200909_RedeBundestagspraesidentSchaeuble.pdf.

21 The authors first raised this question in 2016, in Bastian Giegerich and Maximilian Terhalle, 'The Munich Consensus and the Purpose of German Power', *Survival: Global Politics and Strategy*, vol. 58, no. 2, April–May 2016, pp. 155–66. For the wider debate, see Hans Kundnani, *The Paradox of German Power* (London: C. Hurst & Co., 2014); Leon Mangasarian and Jan Techau, *Führungsmacht Deutschland: Strategie ohne Angst und Anmaßung* [Leading Power Germany: Strategy Without Fear and Presumption]

(Munich: dtv Verlagsgesellschaft, 2017); Christoph von Marschall, *Wir Verstehen die Welt Nicht Mehr: Deutschlands Entfremdung von Seinen Freunden* [We No Longer Understand the World: Germany's Alienation From Its Friends] (Frei-

burg: Verlag Herder, 2018); and Wilfried von Bredow, *Armee Ohne Auftrag: Die Bundeswehr und die Deutsche Sicherheitspolitik* [Army Without a Mission: The Bundeswehr and German Security Policy] (Zurich: Orell Füssli, 2020).

Chapter One

1   John Kampfner, *Why the Germans Do it Better: Notes From a Grown-Up Country* (London: Atlantic Books, 2020), chapters 1–4.

2   Ulrich Schlie, 'Deutsche Sicherheitspolitik Seit 1990: Auf der Suche Nach Einer Strategie' [German Security Policy Since 1990: In Search of a Strategy], *SIRIUS – Zeitschrift für Strategische Analysen*, vol. 4, no. 3, June 2020, pp. 304–14.

3   Michael Howard, 'Book Review: Verteidigung oder Vergeltung (1961)', in *A Historical Sensibility: Sir Michael Howard and The International Institute for Strategic Studies, 1958–2019*, Adelphi 472–474 (Abingdon: Routledge for the IISS, 2020), pp. 43–6, especially p. 44.

4   For example, *The Economist* has argued that 'outsiders, including in the United States, still lament Germany's utter lack of strategic culture'. See 'Germany Is Not About to Invigorate Europe', *The Economist*, 7 December 2017, https://www.economist.com/europe/2017/12/07/germany-is-not-about-to-reinvigorate-the-eu.

5   Ellis S. Krauss and Hanns W. Maull, 'Germany, Japan and the Fate of International Order', *Survival: Global Politics and Strategy*, vol. 62, no. 3, June–July 2020, pp. 159–78, especially pp.

161 and 164.

6   Jan Techau, '"Das Militär ist Keine Lösung"' [The Military is Not a Solution], *Internationale Politik*, issue 6, November/December 2019, p. 15, https://internationalepolitik.de/de/das-militaer-ist-keine-loesung.

7   Stefan Kornelius, 'Pazifismus Mit der Keule' [Pacifism With a Club], *Süddeutsche Zeitung*, 18 December 2020, https://www-sueddeutsche-de.cdn.ampproject.org/c/s/www.sueddeutsche.de/meinung/verteidigung-pazifismus-mit-der-keule-1.5152727!amp.

8   Michael Howard, *The Lessons of History* (Oxford: Clarendon Press, 1991), p. 13.

9   See Graham Allison, *Destined for War: Can America and China Escape Thucydides's Trap?* (Boston, MA: Houghton Mifflin Harcourt, 2017), pp. 55–88.

10 On the success in Germany of Christopher Clark's *The Sleepwalkers* (2012), including Merkel's suggestions that her cabinet ministers read the book, see Jamie Dettmer, 'Europe's Liberals Fear Continent Facing End-of-Era Moment', Voice of America, 3 September 2018, https://www.voanews.com/europe/europes-liberals-fear-continent-facing-end-era-moment; and Jeevan Vasagar, 'Best-Seller List Reveals German Desire to Reassess Great

War', *Financial Times*, 17 January 2014, https://www.ft.com/content/5fdf9fba-7f57-11e3-b6a7-00144feabdco. Merkel's own interest in Clark's argument may be based less on a desire for Germany to avoid the primary responsibility for the First World War than a concern that the contemporary international system may similarly spin out of control. For a critical response to Clark's thesis, see John C.G. Röhl, 'Goodbye to All That (Again)? The Fischer Thesis, the New Revisionism and the Meaning of the First World War', *International Affairs*, vol. 91, no. 1, January 2015, pp. 153–66.

11 See, for example, Omer Bartov, *Hitler's Army: Soldiers, Nazis, and War in the Third Reich* (Oxford: Oxford University Press, 1991); and Sönke Neitzel and Harald Welzer, *Soldiers: German POWs on Fighting, Killing, and Dying* (New York: Vintage Books, 2013).

12 NATO, 'Lord Ismay', https://www.nato.int/cps/us/natohq/declassified_137930.htm.

13 Josef Joffe, 'Once More: The German Question', *Survival: Global Politics and Strategy*, vol. 32, no. 2, April–May 1990, pp. 129–40, especially p. 130.

14 IISS, *Strategic Survey 1990–1991* (London: Brassey's for the IISS, 1991), p. 173.

15 Joffe, 'Once More: The German Question', p. 136 (emphasis in original).

16 Hanns W. Maull, 'Multilateralismus in der Deutschen Außenpolitik' [Multilateralism in German Foreign Policy – A Balance Sheet], *SIRIUS – Zeitschrift für Strategische Analysen*, vol. 4, no. 3, June 2020, pp. 258–75.

17 Krauss and Maull, 'Germany, Japan and the Fate of International Order', pp. 159–78.

18 Ben Barry, *Blood, Metal and Dust: How Victory Turned into Defeat in Afghanistan and Iraq* (Oxford: Osprey Publishing, 2020).

19 Timo Graf, 'Wahrnehmungen der Bilateralen Beziehungen zu China, Russland und den USA' [Perceptions of Bilateral Relations With China, Russia and the USA], in Markus Steinbrecher et al., *Sicherheits- und verteidigungspolitisches Meinungsbild in der Bundesrepublik Deutschland: Ergebnisse und Analysen der Bevölkerungsbefragung 2020* [Security and Defence Policy Opinions in the Federal Republic of Germany: Results and Analysis of the 2020 Population Survey], Forschungsbericht 128 [Research Report 128], Zentrum für Militärgeschichte und Sozialwissenschaften der Bundeswehr [Center for Military History and Social Sciences of the Bundeswehr], March 2021, pp. 74–89, https://www.bundeswehr.de/resource/blob/5036360/dd413dbbd10610484755c6f4fbfbaa93/download-fober-128-data.pdf.

20 Jochen Thies, 'Die Gute Alte Zeit Kommt Nicht Wieder: Die CDU/CSU Muss Aus Ihrem Außenpolitischen Schlaf Erwachen' [The Good Old Days Won't Come Back: The CDU/CSU Has to Wake Up From Its Foreign Policy Slumber], *Internationale Politik*, issue 4, April 2008, pp. 84–7, https://internationalepolitik.de/de/die-gute-alte-zeit-kommt-nicht-wieder; and Melanie Amann et al., 'Der Riss' [The Crack], *Der Spiegel*, 4 May 2018, https://www.spiegel.de/politik/der-riss-a-71d6ea81-0002-0001-0000-000157183899.

21 For arguments that seek to continue building bridges for Russia, see Wolfgang Büchele, 'Begrüßung des Vorsitzenden des Ost-Ausschusses-Osteuropavereins der Deutschen

Wirtschaft: Unternehmergespräch Mit Staatspräsident Vladimir Putin' [Welcome From the Chairman of the German Committee on Eastern European Economic Relations: Business Discussion With President Vladimir Putin], 1 November 2018, https://www.ost-ausschuss.de/sites/default/files/pm_pdf/WB_Statement%20Putin%20in%20Moskau-final.pdf; and Matthias Platzeck, *Wir Brauchen eine Neue Ostpolitik. Russland als Partner* [We Need a New Ostpolitik: Russia as a Partner] (Berlin: Propyläen Verlag, 2020).

22 The writer Nora Krug has spoken of Germany's need to move beyond 'guilt' for its past and fulfil its 'responsibility' to 'defend our democracy', albeit primarily in a domestic context. See Elizabeth Grenier, 'Nora Krug: Replacing German "Guilt" With "Responsibility" to Defend Democracy', Deutsche Welle, 9 August 2019, https://www.dw.com/en/nora-krug-replacing-german-guilt-with-responsibility-to-defend-democracy/a-49960409. For a recent study that traces the evolution of German strategic culture from guilt to responsibility, see Antti Seppo, *From Guilt to Responsibility and Beyond: The Evolution of German Strategic Culture after the End of the Cold War* (Berlin: Berliner Wissenschafts-Verlag, 2021).

23 Angela Merkel, 'Regierungserklärung von Bundeskanzlerin Merkel' [Government Statement by Chancellor Merkel], 13 March 2014, https://www.bundeskanzlerin.de/bkin-de/aktuelles/regierungserklaerung-von-bundeskanzlerin-merkel-443682.

24 George Packer, 'The Quiet German', *New Yorker*, 1 December 2014, https://www.newyorker.com/

magazine/2014/12/01/quiet-german.

25 Kate Brady, 'Außenpolitik Könnte 2020 die Deutsche Regierung Spalten' [Foreign Policy Could Split the German Government in 2020], Deutsche Welle, 24 December 2019, https://www.dw.com/de/au%C3%9Fenpolitik-k%C3%B6nnte-2020-die-deutsche-regierung-spalten/a-51619062.

26 Wissenschaftliche Dienste des Deutschen Bundestages [Scientific Services of the German Bundestag], 'Durchsetzung der Richtlinienkompetenz des Bundeskanzlers' [Enforcement of the Federal Chancellor's Authority to Issue Guidelines], WD 3 – 3000 – 242/18, 29 June 2018, https://www.bundestag.de/resource/blob/568248/39fce9d558f7ae1dda-ec783d7f47723d/WD-3-242-18-pdf-data.pdf. Those who are less sympathetic to Merkel's position may argue that she could have offered her coalition partner more concessions in non-defence-related issues so that, in turn, she could have gained a considerably freer hand in defence-related matters, and the fact that she did not reflects more on her political choices than any legal and constitutional constraints.

27 Heribert Dieter, 'Ein Schwieriger Partner: Deutschlands Eigennützige Außenpolitik' [A Difficult Partner: Germany's Self-Serving Foreign Policy], *SIRIUS – Zeitschrift für Strategische Analysen*, vol. 4, no. 3, June 2020, pp. 245–57.

28 Philipp Rotmann, Sarah Bressan and Sarah Brockmeier, 'Neue Erwartungen: Generation Z und der Einstellungswandel zur Außenpolitik' [New Expectations: Generation Z and Changing Attitudes on German Foreign Policy], Global Public Policy Institute, May 2020, https://www.gppi.net/media/Rotmann_Bressan_Brock-

meier_2020_Neue-Erwartungen_GenZ.pdf.

29 Joachim Gauck, 'Germany's Role in the World: Reflections on Responsibility, Norms and Alliances', speech by Federal President Joachim Gauck to open 50th Munich Security Conference, 31 January 2014, https://www.bundespraesident.de/SharedDocs/Reden/EN/JoachimGauck/Reden/2014/140131-Munich-Security-Conference.html.

30 See Deutscher Akademischer Austauschdienst Hochschulkompass [German Academic Exchange Service University Compass] database, https://www2.daad.de/deutschland/studienangebote/studiengang/de/.

31 The DAAD funds a visiting professorship of 'Strategic Studies' at the Johns Hopkins University School of Advanced International Studies and one of 'Strategy, Diplomacy, and International Security Policy' at the Interdisciplinary Centre (IDC) in Herzliya, Israel. See German Federal Foreign Office, German Academic Exchange Service and Johns Hopkins University's School of Advanced International Studies, 'Inaugural Helmut Schmidt Professor and Five Postdoctoral Fellows, Program on "The United States, Europe, and World Order"', 3 October 2018, https://www2.daad.de/presse/pressemitteilungen/en/66700-inaugural-helmut-schmidt-professor-and-five-postdoctoral-fellows-program-on-the-united-states-europe-and-world-order/; and German Academic Exchange Service, 'Israel – The Interdisciplinary Center (IDC), Lauder School of Government, Diplomacy and Strategy, Herzliya (Langzeitdozentur)', https://www2.daad.de/ausland/lehren/daadlektoren/de/16886-freie-lektorate-und-dozenturen/?s=1&projektid=57575993&page=1.

32 Of course, this is not to suggest that the global-governance literature in international relations is essentially German, as it is heavily connected to US scholarship on institutions and norms. Rather, the starting point expressed here is that this school of thinking holds a quasi-hegemonic position in the relevant academic discussions within Germany.

33 One of the authors provided an in-depth analysis on this topic in 2015. See Maximilian Terhalle, 'Warum das *Governance*-Axiom Gescheitert ist: Eine Notwendige Kritik' [Why the *Governance*-Axiom Failed: A Necessary Criticism], reprinted in *idem*, *Strategie Als Beruf: Überlegungen Zu Strategie, Weltordnung und Strategic Studies* [Strategy as a Profession: Reflections on Strategy, World Order and Strategic Studies] (Marburg: Tectum Verlag, 2020), chapter 19, especially pp. 240–2; and *idem*, *The Transition of Global Order: Legitimacy and Contestation* (London: Palgrave Macmillan, 2015), pp. 26–56.

34 James G. March and Johan P. Olsen, 'The New Institutionalism: Organizational Factors in Political Life', *American Political Science Review*, vol. 78, no. 3, September 1984, p. 741.

35 Deutsche Forschungsgemeinschaft [German Research Foundation], 'Jahresbericht 2019: Aufgaben und Ergebnisse' [Annual Report 2019: Tasks and Results], July 2020, pp. 240–50, https://www.dfg.de/download/pdf/dfg_im_profil/geschaeftsstelle/publikationen/dfg_jb2019.pdf.

36 VolkswagenStiftung [Volkswagen Foundation], 'Anlagestrategie' [Investment

Strategy], 2020, https://www.volkswagenstiftung.de/stiftung/vermoegen/anlagestrategie.

37 Fritz Thyssen Stiftung [Fritz Thyssen Foundation], 'Zahlen, Daten, Fakten: Die Bewilligten Mittel 2019' [Numbers, Data, Facts: Approved Funds for 2019], 2020, https://www.fritz-thyssen-stiftung.de/ueber-uns/allgemeines/zahlen-daten-fakten/; Robert Bosch Stiftung [Robert Bosch Foundation], '2019 Report', July 2020, https://www.bosch-stiftung.de/sites/default/files/publications/pdf/2020-07/Robert_Bosch_Stiftung_Report_2019_EN.pdf; and Gerda Henkel Stiftung [Gerda Henkel Foundation], 'Die Stiftung: Daten und Zahlen' [The Foundation: Facts and Figures], March 2020, https://www.gerda-henkel-stiftung.de/daten_zahlen.

38 As they are negligible in terms of security-related discussions, our analysis does not include the political foundations at the radical-left end of the political spectrum (Die Linke, Rosa-Luxemburg-Stiftung), nor at the radical-right end (AfD, Desiderius-Erasmus-Stiftung). MERICS, a China-focused think tank based in Berlin, continues to retain its well-recognised status as a country-specific think tank, which traditionally possesses less expertise in security- and strategy-related questions that pertain to other states.

39 Christoph Bertram and Christiane Hoffmann, 'Research and Advice in Foreign and Security Policy: An Analysis of the German Think Tank Landscape', Robert Bosch Stiftung and Stiftung Mercator [Robert Bosch Foundation and the Mercator Foundation], September 2020, p. 33, https://www.bosch-stiftung.de/sites/default/files/publications/pdf/2020-09/Research%20and%20advice%20in%20foreign%20and%20security%20policy.pdf.

Chapter Two

1 Annegret Kramp-Karrenbauer, 'Speech by AKK: Presentation of the Steuben Schurz Media Award', 26 October 2020, https://www.bmvg.de/en/news/speech-akk-presentation-steuben-schurz-media-award-3856630.

2 Angela Merkel, 'Bericht der Vorsitzenden der CDU Deutschlands, Bundeskanzlerin Dr. Angela Merkel MdB' [Report of the Chairwoman of the CDU of Germany, Federal Chancellor Dr Angela Merkel MdB], 29 Parteitag der CDU Deutschlands [29th Party Congress of the CDU in Germany], 6–7 December 2016, https://www.cdu.de/system/tdf/media/dokumente/bericht-cdu-vorsitzende-merkel-2016.pdf?file=1.

3 Christian Mölling, 'Vom Flickenteppich Deutscher Sicherheitspolitik' [Of the Patchwork that is German Security Policy], Internationale Politik, issue 5, September/October 2020, pp. 79–83, https://internationalepolitik.de/de/vom-flickenteppich-deutscher-sicherheitspolitik.

4 IISS, The Military Balance 2016 (Abingdon: Routledge for the IISS, 2016), p. 24.

5 Sönke Neitzel, Deutsche Krieger: Vom Kaiserreich zur Berliner Republik – Eine

Militärgeschichte [German Warriors: From the German Empire to the Berlin Republic – A Military History] (Berlin: Propyläen Verlag, 2020), p. 11. The professional identity of soldiers as warriors may thus be lacking in some parts of the armed forces as a result of this discourse, but also because the professional reality of serving personnel, including on international crisis-management operations, will vary, for example between those who spend their tour more or less entirely on base and those who do not. See Anja Seifert, '"Generation Einsatz"' [Generation Operation], *Aus Politik und Zeitgeschichte*, vol. 63, 44/2013, 28 October 2013, pp. 11–16, https://www.bpb.de/apuz/170804/generation-einsatz.

6 Oliver Krause, 'Sönke Neitzel im Interview: "Die Bundeswehr Wird Nicht als Kampftruppe Anerkannt"' [Interview With Sönke Neitzel: 'The Bundeswehr is Not Recognized as a Combat Force'], Deutscher Bundeswehrverband [German Armed Forces Association], 1 August 2020, https://www.dbwv.de/aktuelle-themen/blickpunkt/beitrag/soenke-neitzel-im-interview-die-bundeswehr-wird-nicht-als-kampftruppe-anerkannt/; and Schlie, 'Deutsche Sicherheitspolitik Seit 1990: Auf der Suche Nach Einer Strategie' [German Security Policy Since 1990: In Search of a Strategy], p. 306.

7 Wolfgang Ischinger, *Welt in Gefahr: Deutschland und Europa in Unsicheren Zeiten* [World in Danger: Germany and Europe in Uncertain Times] (Berlin: Econ Verlag, 2018), p. 160. See also Ischinger's interview in *Der Spiegel* where he argues that Germany's insistence, if generalised, that there are no military solutions to crises is misguided: '"Es gilt das Recht des Stärkeren": Spiegel-Gespräch mit Wolfgang Ischinger' ['The Law of the Fittest Applies': Spiegel Interview With Wolfgang Ischinger], *Der Spiegel*, no. 36, 28 August 2020, https://magazin.spiegel.de/SP/2020/36/172728797/index.html.

8 Frank-Walter Steinmeier, 'Deutschlands Chance' [Germany's Opportunity], *Frankfurter Allgemeine Zeitung*, 8 November 2020, https://www.faz.net/aktuell/politik/von-trump-zu-biden/beitrag-des-bundespraesidenten-fuer-die-f-a-z-deutschlands-chance-17042243.html.

9 Horst Köhler, 'Einsatz für Freiheit und Sicherheit: Rede von Bundespräsident Horst Köhler bei der Kommandeurtagung der Bundeswehr in Bonn' [Commitment to Freedom and Security: Speech by Federal President Horst Köhler at the Commanders' Meeting of the Bundeswehr in Bonn], Der Bundespräsident [The Federal President], 10 October 2005, https://www.bundespraesident.de/SharedDocs/Reden/DE/Horst-Koehler/Reden/2005/10/20051010_Rede.html.

10 Steinbrecher et al., *Sicherheits- und verteidigungspolitisches Meinungsbild in der Bundesrepublik Deutschland: Ergebnisse und Analysen der Bevölkerungsbefragung 2020* [Security and Defence Policy Opinions in the Federal Republic of Germany: Results and Analysis of the 2020 Population Survey], pp. 126 (general attitude) and 250 (air policing), https://www.bundeswehr.de/resource/blob/5036360/dd413dbbd10610484755c6f4fbfbaa93/download-fober-128-data.pdf.

11 *Ibid.*, p. 251.

12 *Ibid.*, pp. 78 and 203.

13 *Ibid.*, p. 81.

14 *Ibid.*, p. 54.

15   For information on current and completed operations, see Bundeswehr, 'Aktuelle Einsätze der Bundeswehr' [Current Operations of the Bundeswehr], https://www.bundeswehr.de/de/einsaetze-bundeswehr. See also IISS, *European Military Capabilities: Building Armed Forces for Modern Operations: An IISS Strategic Dossier* (London: IISS, 2008), p. 162.

16   See Arthur Hoffmann and Kerry Longhurst, 'German Strategic Culture and the Changing Role of the *Bundeswehr*', *WeltTrends*, vol. 22, Spring 1999, pp. 145–62, https://publishup.uni-potsdam.de/opus4-ubp/frontdoor/deliver/index/docId/1065/file/22_fb_longhurst.pdf; Jeffrey S. Lantis, *Strategic Dilemmas and the Evolution of German Foreign Policy Since Unification* (Westport, CT: Praeger Publishers, 2002); and Scott Erb, *German Foreign Policy: Navigating a New Era* (Boulder, CO: Lynne Rienner Publishers, 2003).

17   Neitzel, *Deutsche Krieger: Vom Kaiserreich zur Berliner Republik – Eine Militärgeschichte* [German Warriors: From the German Empire to the Berlin Republic – A Military History], p. 444; and Marco Overhaus, 'Zwischen Kooperativer Sicherheit und Militärischer Interventionsfähigkeit – Rot-Grüne Sicherheitspolitik im Rahmen von ESVP und NATO' [Between Cooperative Security and Military Interventions – Red-Green Security Policy Within the Framework of ESDP and NATO], in Hanns W. Maull, Sebastian Harnisch and Constantin Grund (eds), *Deutschland im Abseits? Rot-Grüne Außenpolitik 1998–2003* [Germany Sidelined? Red-Green Foreign Policy 1998–2003] (Baden-Baden: Nomos Verlagsgesellschaft, 2003), pp. 49–63.

18   Bastian Giegerich, *European Security and Strategic Culture: National Responses to the EU's Security and Defence Policy, Düsseldorfer Schriften zu Internationaler Politik und Völkerrecht* [Düsseldorf Writings on International Politics and International Law], vol. 1 (Baden-Baden: Nomos Verlagsgesellschaft, 2006), p. 142; Krause, 'Sönke Neitzel im Interview: "Die Bundeswehr Wird Nicht als Kampftruppe Anerkannt"' [Interview With Sönke Neitzel: 'The Bundeswehr is Not Recognized as a Combat Force']; and Thorsten Benner, 'Gegen das Geschwurbel' [Against the Swirl], *Internationale Politik*, issue 2, March/April 2019, pp. 14–17, https://internationalepolitik.de/de/gegen-das-geschwurbel.

19   Eric Sangar, 'The Weight of the Past(s): The Impact of the Bundeswehr's Use of Historical Experience on Strategy-Making in Afghanistan', *Journal of Strategic Studies*, vol. 38, no. 4, May 2015, pp. 411–44; Bastian Giegerich and Stéfanie von Hlatky, 'Experiences May Vary: NATO and Cultural Interoperability in Afghanistan', *Armed Forces & Society*, vol. 46, no. 3, July 2020, pp. 495–516, especially pp. 505–7; and Krause, 'Sönke Neitzel im Interview: "Die Bundeswehr Wird Nicht als Kampftruppe Anerkannt"' [Interview With Sönke Neitzel: 'The Bundeswehr is Not Recognized as a Combat Force'].

20   Christoph von Marschall and Mathias Müller von Blumencron, 'Ex-Verteidigungsminister Volker Rühe: "Guttenberg Hat die Bundeswehr Zerstört"' [Ex-Defence Minister Volker Rühe: 'Guttenberg Destroyed the Bundeswehr'], *Der Tagesspiegel*, 10 February 2019, https://www.tagesspiegel.de/politik/ex-verteidigungsminister-vol-

ker-ruehe-guttenberg-hat-die-bundeswehr-zerstoert/23968822-all.html.

21 Wilfried von Bredow, 'Germany in Afghanistan: The Pitfalls of Peace-Building in National and International Perspective', *Res Militaris*, vol. 2, no. 1, Autumn 2011, http://www.resmilitaris.net/ressources/10150/00/7_res_militaris_article_von_bredow_germany_in_afghanistan.pdf.

22 See Deutscher Bundestag [German Bundestag], 'Unterrichtung durch die Kommission zur Überprüfung und Sicherung der Parlamentsrechte bei der Mandatierung von Auslandseinsätzen der Bundeswehr – Abschlussbericht der Kommission [Briefing by the Comission for the Review and Safeguarding of Parliamentary Rights When Mandating Foreign Deployments of the Bundeswehr – Final Report of the Commission], Drucksache 18/5000 [Printed Matter 18/5000], 16 June 2015, https://dip21.bundestag.de/dip21/btd/18/050/1805000.pdf; Ekkehard Brose, 'Europäische Handlungsfähigkeit Braucht Pragmatismus – Auch im Deutschen Bundestag [European Capacity to Act Needs Pragmatism – Also in the German Bundestag], Anmerkungen zur sicherheitspolitischen Debatte [Comments on the Security Policy Debate], no. 3/20, Bundesakademie für Sicherheitspolitik [Federal Academy for Security Policy], 4 February 2020, https://www.baks.bund.de/sites/baks010/files/angebakst_20-3_0.pdf; and Jäger, 'Neue Strategische Lage: Deutschland Sollte Interventionsfähig Sein' [New Strategic Situation: Germany Should Be Able to Intervene].

23 Thorsten Junghold and Jacques Schuster, 'Generalinspekteur sieht Nato-Ziele Durch Corona Gefähr-det' [Inspector General Views NATO Goals as At Risk From Corona], *Die Welt*, 3 January 2021, https://www.welt.de/politik/deutschland/article223639720/Bundeswehr-Generalinspekteur-Eberhard-Zorn-sieht-Nato-Ziele-gefaehrdet.html.

24 Matthias Gebauer and Konstantin von Hammerstein, 'Der Bundeswehr Geht das Geld Aus' [The Bundeswehr Is Running Out of Money], *Der Spiegel*, 5 February 2021, https://www.spiegel.de/politik/deutschland/der-bundeswehr-geht-das-geld-aus-geheime-finanzbedarfsanalyse-2022-a-00000000-0002-0001-0000-000175196797.

25 Deutscher Bundestag [German Bundestag], 'Unterrichtung Durch die Wehrbeauftragte' [Briefing by the Armed Forces Commissioner], Jahresbericht 2020 (62. Bericht) [Annual Report 2020 (62nd Report)], Durcksache 19/26600 [Printed Matter 19/26600], 23 February 2021, p. 6, https://dip21.bundestag.de/dip21/btd/19/266/1926600.pdf.

26 Bundesministerium der Verteidigung [Federal Ministry of Defence], 'Weißbuch 1994: Weißbuch zur Sicherheit der Bundesrepublik Deutschland und zur Lage und Zukunft der Bundeswehr' [White Paper 1994: White Paper on the Security of the Federal Republic of Germany and the Situation and Future of the Bundeswehr], 1994, paragraph 302.

27 Rudolf Scharping and Bundesministerium der Verteidigung [Federal Ministry of Defence], 'Die Bundeswehr – sicher ins 21. Jahrhundert: Eckpfeiler für eine Erneuerung von Grund auf' [The Bundeswehr – Securely into the 21st Century: Cornerstones for a Renewal From the Ground Up], 2000.

28 Peter Struck, 'Defence Policy Guidelines', Bundesministerium der Verteidi-

gung [Federal Ministry of Defence], 21 May 2003, https://www.files.ethz.ch/isn/157025/Germany_English2003.pdf.

29 Federal Ministry of Defence, 'White Paper 2006 on German Security Policy and the Future of the Bundeswehr', 2006, p. 9, https://issat.dcaf.ch/content/download/17423/203638/version/2/file/Germany_White_Paper_2006.pdf.

30 The Federal Government, 'White Paper 2016 on German Security Policy and the Future of the Bundeswehr', 13 July 2016, pp. 91–3, https://issat.dcaf.ch/download/111704/2027268/2016%20White%20Paper.pdf.

31 See, for example, Johannes Varwick, 'Von Leistungsgrenzen und Trendwenden: Was Soll und Kann die Bundeswehr?' [Of Performance Limits and Trend Reversals: What Should and Can the Bundeswehr Do?], *Aus Politik und Zeitgeschichte*, vol. 70, 16–17/2020, 14 April 2020, pp. 31–7, https://www.bpb.de/apuz/307664/von-leistungs-grenzen-und-trendwenden-was-soll-und-kann-die-bundeswehr; and Rainer Meyer zum Felde, 'Deutsche Verteidigungspolitik – Versäumnisse und Nicht Eingehaltene Versprechen' [German Defence Policy – Failures and Promises Not Kept], *SIRIUS – Zeitschrift für Strategische Analysen*, vol. 4, no. 3, June 2020, pp. 315–32, https://www.degruyter.com/document/doi/10.1515/sirius-2020-3007/html.

32 Deutscher Bundestag [German Bundestag], 'Unterrichtung Durch den Wehrbeauftragten' [Briefing From the Parliamentary Commissioner for the Armed Forces], Jahresbericht 2019 (61. Bericht) [Annual Report 2019 (61st Report)], Drucksache 19/16500 [Printed Matter 19/16500], 28 January 2020, pp. 5 and 42, https://dip21.bundestag.de/dip21/btd/19/165/1916500.

pdf. It is important to recognise that, thanks to the existence of this commissioner, Germany is more transparent than other NATO and EU nations with regard to these questions. A defence official from another major NATO country only half-jokingly suggested to one of the authors of this book in early 2020 that they were grateful for the German commissioner's reports (which are available in English) because the situation they portrayed was so dire that it distracted from their own country's problems.

33 Johannes Leithäuser and Marco Seliger, 'Bis Zu den Sternen' [To the Stars], *Frankfurter Allgemeine Zeitung*, 19 April 2017.

34 Bastian Giegerich, 'Große Aufgaben, Kleine Schritte: Der Weg für Einen Erfolgreichen Neuaufbau der Bundeswehr Ist Abgesteckt' [Big Tasks, Small Steps: The Path for a Successful Reconstruction of the Bundeswehr], *Internationale Politik*, issue 5, September/October 2018, pp. 14–18, https://internationalepolitik.de/de/grosse-aufgaben-kleine-schritte.

35 Eberhard Zorn, 'Die Anspruchsvollste Aufgabe der Bundeswehr' [The Most Demanding Task of the Bundeswehr], *Frankfurter Allgemeine Zeitung*, 30 September 2020, p. 8.

36 Alfons Mais, 'Stark Sein, um den Frieden zu Bewahren!' [Be Strong to Preserve the Peace!], *InfoBrief Heer*, no. 1, February 2021, pp. 1–4, http://www.fkhev.de/fileadmin/InfoBrief-Heer_01-2021_WEB.pdf.

37 Interessengemeinschaft Deutsche Luftwaffe e.V. [Interest Group of the German Air Force e.V.], '"Die Luftwaffe Befindet sich an einem Tiefpunkt!"' ['The Air Force Is at a Low Point!'], 11 July 2018, https://www.idlw.de/die-luft-waffe-befindet-sich-an-einem-tiefpunkt.

38 Ingo Gerhartz, 'German Air Force Chief: The Service Is Undergoing Upgrades to Meet Future Challenges', *Defense News*, 11 January 2021, https://www.defense news.com/outlook/2021/01/11/german-air-force-chief-the-service-is-under going-upgrades-to-meet-future-chal lenges/.

39 Andreas Krause, 'Rede vor den Angehörigen der Crew 2020' [Address to the Members of the Crew 2020], 20 January 2021, p. 7, https://www.bundeswehr. de/resource/blob/5020882/162426094eb 6486a19b7417900716272/file.

40 Andreas Krause, 'Ansprache: 60. Historisch Taktische Tagung' [Address: 60th Historical Tactical Conference], 9 January 2020, pp. 23–4, https:// w w w . b u n d e s w e h r . d e / r e s o u r c e / blob/169242/a7af7af8ea2ce1aba754c-f80a59880c6/ansprache-des-inspekteurs-der-marine-zur-60-historisch-taktischen-tagung-data.pdf.

41 Hans-Uwe Mergener, 'Fregatte mit Kurs Indopazifik?' [Frigate Heading Towards the Indo-Pacific?], Marine-Forum, 3 March 2021, https://marine-forum.online/fregatte-mit-kurs-indo-pazifik/; and Gerhartz, 'German Air Force Chief: The Service is Undergoing Upgrades to Meet Future Challenges'.

42 John Chipman, 'Shifting weight of military power', IISS Analysis, 29 January 2018, https://www.iiss.org/blogs/ analysis/2018/01/shifting-weight.

43 All recent data: IISS, *The Military Balance* and the Military Balance+ database, https://milbalplus.iiss.org/, accessed April 2021.

44 Karl-Heinz Kamp, 'Myths Surrounding the Two Percent Debate – on NATO defence spending', Security Policy Working Paper no. 9/2019, Bundesakademie für Sicherheitspolitik [Federal Academy for Security Policy], https://

www.baks.bund.de/sites/baks010/ files/working_paper_2019_9.pdf.

45 Angela Merkel, 'Speech by Federal Chancellor Dr Angela Merkel on 16 February 2019 at the 55th Munich Security Conference', 16 February 2019, https://www.bundesregierung. de/breg-en/news/speech-by-federal-chancellor-dr-angela-merkel-on-16-february-2019-at-the-55th-munich-security-conference-1582318.

46 Meyer zum Felde, 'Deutsche Verteidigungspolitik – Versäumnisse und Nicht Eingehaltene Versprechen' [German Defence Policy – Failures and Promises Not Kept], p. 322, https://www. degruyter.com/document/doi/10.1515/ sirius-2020-3007/html; see also Karl-Heinz Kamp, 'Mythen der Zwei-Prozent-Debatte: Zur Diskussion um die NATO-Verteidigungsausgaben' [Myths of the Two-Percent Debate: On the Discussion of NATO Defence Spending], Arbeitspapier Sicherheitspolitik no. 9/2019 [Security Policy Working Paper no. 9/2019], Bundesakademie für Sicherheitspolitik [Federal Academy for Security Policy], p. 5, https:// www.baks.bund.de/de/arbeitspa piere/2019/mythen-der-zwei-pro zent-debatte-zur-diskussion-um-die-nato-verteidigungsausgaben.

47 Gebauer and von Hammerstein, 'Der Bundeswehr Geht das Geld Aus' [The Bundeswehr Is Running Out of Money]; and Matthias Gebauer and Konstantin von Hammerstein, 'Kramp-Karrenbauer Soll mit 42 Milliarden Euro Weniger Auskommen' [Kramp-Karrenbauer To Manage With 42 Billion Euros Less], *Der Spiegel*, 19 March 2021, https:// www.spiegel.de/politik/deutschland/ bundeswehr-annegret-kramp-kar renbauer-soll-mit-42-milliarden-euro-weniger-auskommen-a-6c1356d1-

0002-0001-0000-000176418826?context=issue.

48 Thomas Wiegold, 'Lange Liste Für die Rüstungsbeschaffung – und Lange Liste der Projekte Ohne Geld' [Long List for Arms Procurement – and Long List of Projects Without Money], Augen Geradeaus, 3 February 2021, https://augengeradeaus.net/2021/02/lange-liste-fuer-die-ruestungsbeschaffung-und-lange-liste-der-projekte-ohne-geld/comment-page-1/.

49 Peter Carsten, 'Die Bundeswehr hat Probleme, ihren Etat richtig zu investieren' [The Bundeswehr Has Problems Investing Its Budget Properly], *Frankfurter Allgemeine Zeitung*, 8 December 2020, https://www.faz.net/aktuell/politik/inland/bundesrechnungshof-die-geldprobleme-der-bundeswehr-17091753.html; Nikolaus Doll, 'Hier hat Deutschland Millionen an Steuergeldern Verschwendet' [Germany Has Wasted Millions in Taxpayers' Money], *Die Welt*, 24 April 2018, https://www.welt.de/wirtschaft/article175744431/Steuern-Bundeswehr-gilt-als-grosser-Verschwender.html; and 'Von der Leyen Lässt 400 Millionen Euro Verfallen' [Von der Leyen Lets 400 Mil-

lion Euros Expire], *Merkur*, 5 October 2014, https://www.merkur.de/politik/leyen-laesst-millionen-euro-verfallen-zr-4044320.html.

50 See von Marschall and Müller von Blumencron, 'Ex-Verteidigungsminister Volker Rühe: "Guttenberg Hat die Bundeswehr Zerstört"' [Ex-Defence Minister Volker Rühe: 'Guttenberg Destroyed the Bundeswehr'].

51 Annegret Kramp-Karrenbauer, 'Rede der Bundesministerin der Verteidigung Annegret Kramp-Karrenbauer an der Helmut–Schmidt–Universität / Universität der Bundeswehr' [Speech of the Federal Minister of Defence Annegret Kramp-Karrenbauer at the Helmut Schmidt University / University of the Federal Armed Forces], Bundesministerium der Verteidigung [Federal Ministry of Defence], 17 November 2020, p. 12, https://www.bmvg.de/resource/blob/4483202/a62307ebef4572c1cff-a40eb91093417/20201117-dl-grundsatzrede-unibwhh-data.pdf; and Varwick, 'Von Leistungsgrenzen und Trendwenden: Was Soll und Kann die Bundeswehr?' [Of Performance Limits and Trend Reversals: What Should and Can the Bundeswehr Do?], p. 37.

Chapter Three

1 For a clear and illuminating interview with General Sir Richard Barrons, see Konstantin von Hammerstein, '"So Können Sie Jedes Europäische Land in Nur 14 Tagen in die Knie Zwingen"' ['This Is How You Can Bring Any European Country to Its

Knees in Just 14 Days'], *Der Spiegel*, 23 May 2020, https://www.spiegel.de/politik/ausland/ex-general-richard-barrons-ueber-den-krieg-der-zukunft-kampfroboter-bekommen-keine-pension-a-058c61c5-e4c2-4845-9d0e-33f3a7a3e4cc.

2 Douglas Barrie et al., 'European Defence Policy in an Era of Renewed Great-Power Competition', IISS and Hanns Seidel Foundation, February 2020, pp. 16–17, https://www.iiss.org/blogs/research-paper/2020/02/the-future-of-european-defence.

3 Douglas Barrie and Bastian Giegerich, 'Buying Yourself Into Trouble: Germany's Procurement Problem', IISS, *Military Balance* blog, 16 December 2020, https://www.iiss.org/blogs/military-balance/2020/12/germany-procurement-problem.

4 See Wilfried von Bredow, *Armee Ohne Auftrag: Die Bundeswehr und die Deutsche Sicherheitspolitik* [Army Without a Mission: The Bundeswehr and German Security Policy] (Zurich: Orell Füssli, 2020).

5 Stephan Löwenstein, 'Sparen bei den Streitkräften? Unruhe in der Bundeswehr nach Guttenbergs Rede' [Cuts in the Armed Forces? Unrest in the Bundeswehr After Guttenberg's Speech], *Frankfurter Allgemeine Zeitung*, 27 May 2010, https://www.faz.net/aktuell/politik/inland/sparen-bei-den-streitkraeften-unruhe-in-der-bundeswehr-nach-guttenbergs-rede-1978191.html?printPagedArticle=true#void.

6 Thomas Wiegold, 'Späte Genugtuung für Guttenberg: Bundeswehr Sparte Mehr als 8 Mrd Euro' [Late Satisfaction for Guttenberg: Bundeswehr Saved More Than 8 Billion Euros], Augen Geradeaus, 25 July 2014, https://augengeradeaus.net/2014/07/spaete-genugtuung-fuer-guttenberg-bundeswehr-sparte-mehr-als-8-mrd-euro/.

7 Conversations between an author of this book and German officials suggested that the paradigm shift introduced in zu Guttenberg's speech was added to the remarks at short notice and without a full assessment of the consequences that may arise from it.

8 Wissenschaftliche Dienste des Deutschen Bundestages [Scientific Services of the German Bundestag], 'Die Neuausrichtung der Bundeswehr – Ziele, Maßnahmen, Herausforderungen' [The Realignment of the Bundeswehr – Goals, Actions, Challenges], WD 2 – 3000 – 040/14, 10 April 2014, pp. 17–18, https://www.bundestag.de/resource/blob/412254/04d0b8db2d14ece3a72d-9b580c9578a6/WD-2-040-14-pdf-data.pdf.

9 Interview with German official, April 2020.

10 IISS Military Balance+ database, https://milbalplus.iiss.org/, accessed April 2021.

11 *Ibid.*

12 KPMG, P3 Group and TaylorWessing, 'Umfassende Bestandsaufnahme und Risikoanalyse Zentraler Rüstungsprojekte: Exzerpt' [Comprehensive Inventory and Risk Analysis of Central Armaments Projects: Summary], 30 September 2014, https://www.bmvg.de/resource/blob/11644/d5cdd057b87a9a9f84dad-eaa72d4ae59/c-06-10-14-download-expertenbericht-zu-ruestungsprojek-ten-uebergeben-data.pdf.

13 IISS Military Balance+ database, https://milbalplus.iiss.org/, accessed April 2021.

14 *Ibid.*

15 See, for example, Dorothee Frank, 'Bundeswehr-Marder Erhalten Saphir Wärmebildzielgeräte' [Bundeswehr's Marder to Receive Saphir Thermal Imaging Aiming Devices], *Behörden Spiegel*, 9 November 2020, https://www.beho-erden-spiegel.de/2020/11/09/bundes-wehr-marder-erhalten-saphir-waer-mebildzielgeraete/.

16 IISS Military Balance+ database, https://milbalplus.iiss.org/, accessed April 2021.

17 Nicholas Fiorenza, 'Germany's F125 Frigate Nordrhein-Westfalen Enters Service', Janes, 16 June 2020, https://www.janes.com/defence-news/news-detail/germanys-f125-frigate-nordrhein-westfalen-enters-service.

18 Deutscher Bundestag [German Bundestag], 'Antwort der Bundesregierung auf die Kleine Anfrage der Abgeordneten Dr. Marcus Faber, Alexander Graf Lambsdorff, Grigorios Aggelidis, Weiterer Abgeordneter und der Fraktion der FDP' [Answer of the Federal Government to the Minor Interpellation of MPs Dr. Marcus Faber, Alexander Graf Lambsdorff, Grigorios Aggelidis, Other MPs and the FDP Parliamentary Group], Drucksache 19/9353 [Printed Matter 19/9353], 9 April 2019, http://dipbt.bundestag.de/dip21/btd/19/093/1909353.pdf.

19 Plans to develop electronic-combat-reconnaissance and suppression-of-enemy-air-defence versions of the Eurofighter were announced at the end of 2019. See Gareth Jennings, 'Airbus Proposes ECR/SEAD Eurofighter, Emphasises German Requirement', Janes, 5 November 2019, https://www.janes.com/defence-news/news-detail/airbus-proposes-ecrsead-eurofighter-emphasises-german-requirement.

20 Matthias Gebauer and Konstantin von Hammerstein, 'Die Radmuttern Werden Nicht Mehr Hergestellt' [The Wheel Nuts Are No Longer Manufactured], Der Spiegel, 10 April 2020, https://www.spiegel.de/politik/deutschland/tornado-flugzeuge-der-bundeswehr-die-radmuttern-werden-gar-nicht-mehr-hergestellt-a-00000000-0002-0001-0000-000170435625?context=issue. See also Douglas Barrie, 'Dogfight Over Berlin: Germany's Tornado Replacement Aspirations', IISS, Military Balance blog, 21 December 2017, https://www.iiss.org/blogs/military-balance/2017/12/berlin; and Douglas Barrie and Bastian Giegerich, 'Berlin and the Bomb', IISS, Military Balance blog, 20 March 2020, https://www.iiss.org/blogs/military-balance/2020/03/germany-tornado-replacement-options.

21 The Christian Democratic Union of Germany, the Christian Social Union in Bavaria and the Free Democratic Party, 'Wachstum. Bildung. Zusammenhalt. Der Koalitionsvertrag Zwischen CDU, CSU und FDP' [Growth. Education. Unity. The Coalition Agreement Between the CDU, CSU and FDP], 26 October 2009, p. 120, https://www.kas.de/c/document_library/get_file?uuid=83dbb842-b2f7-bf99-6180-e65b2de7b4d4&groupId=252038.

22 The Christian Democratic Union of Germany, the Christian Social Union in Bavaria and the Social Democratic Party of Germany, 'Ein Neuer Aufbruch für Europa. Eine Neue Dynamik für Deutschland. Ein Neuer Zusammenhalt für Unser Land: Koalitionsvertrag zwischen CDU, CSU und SPD' [A New Departure for Europe. A New Dynamic for Germany. A New Cohesion for Our Country: Coalition Agreement Between CDU, CSU and SPD], 12 March 2018, p. 148, https://www.bundesregierung.de/resource/blob/656734/847984/5b8bc23590d4cb2892b31c987ad672b7/2018-03-14-koalitionsvertrag-data.pdf.

23 Paul-Anton Krüger and Mike Szymanski, 'Berlin und die Bombe: Ein Offenes Geheimnis' [Berlin and the Bomb: An Open Secret], Süddeutsche Zeitung, 5 May 2020, https://

www.sueddeutsche.de/politik/ atomwaffen-atombombe-1.4897147.

24 Soumitra Dutta, Bruno Lanvin and Sacha Wunsch-Vincent (eds), 'Global Innovation Index 2020: Who Will Finance Innovation?', Cornell University, INSEAD and the World Intellectual Property Organization, September 2020, p. xxxii, https://www.wipo.int/edocs/ pubdocs/en/wipo_pub_gii_2020.pdf.

25 Amy J. Nelson, 'Innovation and Its Discontents: National Models of Military Innovation and the Dual-Use Conundrum', Center for International and Security Studies at School of Public Policy, University of Maryland, July 2020, pp. 4 and 19, https://cissm. umd.edu/sites/default/files/2020-07/ EmergingTechInnovation_063020.pdf.

26 Mölling, 'Vom Flickenteppich Deutscher Sicherheitspolitik' [Of the Patchwork that is German Security Policy], p. 80.

27 Florian Keisinger (Airbus) and Wolfgang Koch (Fraunhofer FKIE), 'Mission', Future Combat Air System, http://www.fcas-forum.eu/mission.

28 The IISS has been a partner organisation in this effort and has received project funding from the German foreign ministry for this purpose. See '2021. Capturing Technology. Rethinking Arms Control', Federal Foreign Office, http:// www.rethinkingarmscontrol.de.

29 Timothy Wright, Douglas Barrie and Bastian Giegerich, 'Multi-Stakeholder Approaches to Arms Control Negotiations: Working With Science and Industry', in Federal Foreign Office, 'Conference Reader: 2020. Capturing Technology. Rethinking Arms Control', November 2020, pp. 47–53, https://rethinkingarmscontrol.de/ wp-content/uploads/2020/10/20-AA-RAC-Reader-2020-10-28-final-korr-kompr.pdf.

30 See '"Eine Gute Erfindung Steigert das Gemeinwohl": Rafael Laguna de la Verde im Gespräch mit Annette Riedel' ['A Good Invention Increases the Common Good': Rafael Laguna de la Vera in Conversation With Annette Riedel], Deutschlandfunk Kultur, 29 February 2020, https://www.deutschland-funkkultur.de/chef-der-agentur-fuer-sprunginnovationen-eine-gute.990. de.html?dram:article_id=471145; Shirley Tay, 'Exclusive: How the German Military Created a Startup Culture', GovInsider, 9 November 2020, https://govinsider.asia/intelligent-gov/ how-the-german-military-created-a-startup-culture-marcel-otto-yon/; 'Offizieller Startschuss für Cyberagentur' [Official Starting Signal for Cyber Agency], Tagesschau, 11 August 2020, https://www.tagesschau.de/inland/ cyberagentur-105.html; and Michael Brauns, 'Universitäten der Bundeswehr gründen DTEC.Bw' [Universities of the Federal Armed Forces Establish DTEC.Bw], Bundeswehr University Munich, 24 September 2020, https://www.unibw.de/home/news/ universitaeten-der-bundeswehr-gruenden-zentrum-fuer-digitalisierungs-und-technologieforschung.

31 Judy Dempsey, 'Why Germany's Soldiers Are Denied Armed Drones', Judy Dempsey's Strategic Europe, Carnegie Europe, 5 January 2021, https://carnegieeurope. eu/strategiceurope/83558?mkt_tok=eyJpIj oiTVdJMVlUZzFNR1kwToRrNSIsInQiO iJZaDVMWm5QZEhYZXF6dTZHdm9Q So1p%E2%80%A6.

32 Bundesverband der Deutschen Sicherheits- und Verteidigungsindustrie [Federal Association of the German Security and Defence Industry], 'Die Deutsche Sicherheits- und Verteidigungsindustrie als Teil Einer Nationalen Sicherheits-

und Verteidigungsvorsorge' [The German Security and Defence Industry as Part of a National Security and Defence Preparedness], 21 June 2017, p. 1, https://www.bdsv.eu/aktuelles/positionspapiere/positionspapier-des-bdsv-zur-thematik-souveraenitaet.html.

33 Krauss-Maffei Wegmann used to be on this list but its revenue is now reported as part of KNDS, which is the holding company it established with France's Nexter Systems. The company is registered in the Netherlands. See 'Top 100 for 2020', *Defense News*, https://people.defensenews.com/top-100/.

34 Die Bundesregierung [Cabinet of Germany], 'Strategy Paper of the Federal Government on Strengthening the Security and Defence Industry', 14 February 2020, https://www.bmwi.de/Redaktion/DE/Downloads/S-T/strategiepapier-staerkung-sicherits-und-verteidigungsindustrie-en.pdf?__blob=publicationFile&v=4.

35 Bastian Giegerich, 'Coopération Franco-Allemande de Sécurité et de Défense et Autonomie Stratégique Européenne' [Franco-German Security and Defence Cooperation and European Strategic Autonomy], *Revue Défense Nationale*, 2019/6 (no. 821), June 2019, pp. 43–9.

36 Detlef Puhl, 'La Coopération en Matière d'Armement Entre la France et l'Allemagne: Un Terrain d'Entente Impossible?' [The Franco-German Armaments Cooperation: An Impossible Agreement?], *Notes de l'Ifri – Visions Franco-Allemandes*, [Ifri Notes – Franco-German Visions] no. 31, November 2020, https://www.ifri.org/fr/publications/notes-de-lifri/visions-franco-allemandes/cooperation-matiere-darmement-entre-france. See also Barbara Kunz, 'Switching Umbrellas in Berlin? The Implications of Franco-German

Nuclear Cooperation', *Washington Quarterly*, vol. 43, no. 3, September 2020, pp. 63–77; and Nelson, 'Innovation and Its Discontents: National Models of Military Innovation and the Dual-Use Conundrum', p. 20.

37 Die Bundesregierung [Cabinet of Germany], 'Strategy Paper of the Federal Government on Strengthening the Security and Defence Industry', 14 February 2020, p. 8, https://www.bmwi.de/Redaktion/DE/Downloads/S-T/strategiepapier-staerkung-sicherits-und-verteidigungsindustrie-en.pdf?__blob=publicationFile&v=4.

38 Ischinger, *Welt in Gefahr: Deutschland und Europa in Unsicheren Zeiten* [World in Danger: Germany and Europe in Uncertain Times], p. 280.

39 Conversations between an author of this paper and German industry representatives, February and April 2020.

40 Thomas Wiegold, 'Deutscher Exportstopp für die Saudis: Großbritannien Warnt Deutschland vor Folgen' [German Export Ban For the Saudis: Great Britain Warns Germany of the Consequences], Augen Geradeaus, 19 February 2019, https://augengeradeaus.net/2019/02/deutscher-exportstopp-fuer-die-saudis-grossbritannien-warnt-deutschland-vor-folgen/. See also Matthias Gebauer and Christoph Schult, 'Großbritannien Wirft Berlin Mangelnde Bündnistreue Vor' [Great Britain Accuses Berlin of Lacking Loyalty to the Alliance], *Der Spiegel*, 19 February 2019, https://www.spiegel.de/politik/deutschland/ruestungsexporte-nach-saudi-arabien-brandbrief-aus-grossbritannien-an-deutschland-a-1253997.html.

41 Anne-Marie Descôtes, 'Vom "German-Free" zum Gegenseitigen Vertrauen' [From 'German-Free' to Mutual Trust], Arbeitspapier Sicherheitspolitik no.

7/2019 [Security Policy Working Paper no. 7/2019], Bundesakademie für Sicherheitspolitik [Federal Academy for Security Policy], https://www.baks.bund.de/sites/baks010/files/arbeitspapier_sicherheitspolitik_2019_7.pdf.

42 See BAE Systems, 'Our Key Markets', https://www.baesystems.com/en/what-we-do/suppliers/our-key-markets.

43 Rick Noack, 'Germany's Ban on Arms Exports to Saudi Arabia Is Having a Bigger Impact Than Expected', *Stars and Stripes*, 19 February 2019, https://www.stripes.com/news/europe/germany-s-ban-on-arms-exports-to-saudi-arabia-is-having-a-bigger-impact-than-expected-1.569265; and Nelson, 'Innovation and Its Discontents: National Models of Military Innovation and the Dual-Use Conundrum', p. 20.

44 Lucie Béraud-Sudreau, 'Building Franco-German Consensus on Arms Exports', *Survival: Global Politics and Strategy*, vol. 61, no. 4, August–September 2019, pp. 79–98, especially p. 80.

45 Matthias Gebauer and Gerald Traufetter, 'Regierung Genehmigt Neue Waffendeals mit Saudi-Arabien' [Government Approves New Arms Deals With Saudi Arabia], *Der Spiegel*, 19 September 2018, https://www.spiegel.de/politik/deutschland/ruestung-bundesregierung-genehmigt-neue-waffen-deals-mit-saudi-arabien-a-1229003.html.

46 Barrie and Giegerich, 'Buying Yourself Into Trouble: Germany's Procurement Problem'; Wissenschaftliche Dienste des Deutschen Bundestages [Scientific Services of the German Bundestag], 'Das Deutsch-Französische Abkommen Vom 21. Oktober 2019 Über Ausfuhrkontrollen im Rüstungsbereich im Lichte des Art. 59 Abs. 2 GG' [The Franco-German Agreement of 21 October 2019 on Export Controls in Arms Policy in Light of Article 59, Paragraph 2 of the Basic Law], WD 2 – 3000 - 122/19, 15 November 2019, pp. 8–9, https://www.bundestag.de/resource/blob/673972/3921230d2453e988b485aae981323a35/WD-2-122-19-pdf-data.pdf; and Federal Office for Economic Affairs and Export Control, 'War Weapons List', https://www.bafa.de/SharedDocs/Downloads/EN/Foreign_Trade/afk_war_weapons_list.html.

Chapter Four

1 Catherine Philp and Didi Tang, 'We Must Confront Threat of China, Says Nato Chief Jens Stoltenberg', *The Times*, 25 March 2021, https://www.thetimes.co.uk/article/we-must-confront-threat-of-china-says-nato-chief-jens-stoltenberg-fv36m2rr5.

2 For the debate concerning the number of deaths for which Mao Zedong may be responsible, see Ian Johnson, 'Who Killed More: Hitler, Stalin, or Mao?', *New York Review of Books*, 5 February 2018, https://www.nybooks.com/daily/2018/02/05/who-killed-more-hitler-stalin-or-mao/. For more recent oppressions committed by the Chinese government, see Sasha Chavkin, 'China Cables: Who Are the Uighurs and Why Mass Detention?', International Consortium of Investigative Journalists, 24 November 2019, https://www.icij.org/investigations/china-cables/china-cables-who-are-the-uighurs-

and-why-mass-detention/?gclid= EAIaIQobChMIuNuRz5S47wIVy-7tCh31Cw31EAMYAiAAEgK9b_D_ BwE; Lea Deuber and Reiko Pinkert, 'Bericht des Auswärtigen Amts beklagt Verfolgung der Uiguren' [Foreign Office Report Complains About Persecution of the Uighurs], *Süddeutsche Zeitung*, 31 January 2020, https://www.sued-deutsche.de/politik/auswaertiges-amt-china-uiguren-verfolgung-1.4779614; and James Landale, 'Uighurs: "Credible case" China Carrying Out Genocide', BBC, 8 February 2021, https://www.bbc.co.uk/news/uk-55973215.

3   Adrienne Klasa et al., 'Russia's Long Arm Reaches to the Right in Europe', *Financial Times*, 23 May 2019, https://www.ft.com/content/48c4bfa6-7ca2-11e9-81d2-f785092ab560; Susi Dennison and Dina Pardijs, 'The World According to Europe's Insurgent Parties: Putin, Migration and People Power', European Council on Foreign Relations, June 2016, https://ecfr.eu/wp-content/uploads/ecfr_181_-_the_world_according_to_europe_insurgent_parties_new.pdf; and Péter Krekó and Lóránt Győri, 'From Russia With Hate: The Kremlin's Support for Violent Extremism in Central Europe', UkraineAlert, Atlantic Council, 17 May 2017, https://www.atlanticcouncil.org/blogs/ukrainealert/from-russia-with-hate-the-kremlin-s-support-for-violent-extremism-in-central-europe/.

4   James Kirchick, 'Russia's Plot Against the West', Politico, 17 March 2017, https://www.politico.eu/article/russia-plot-against-the-west-vladimir-putin-donald-trump-europe/; Lionel Barber, Henry Foy and Alex Barker, 'Vladimir Putin Says Liberalism Has "Become Obsolete"', *Financial Times*, 28 June 2019, https://www.ft.com/content/670039ec-98f3-11e9-9573-ee-

5cbb98ed36; Ivo Daalder, 'Die Unheil-volle Allianz Gegen die Freiheitliche Weltordnung' [The Sinister Alliance Against the Liberal World Order], *Handelsblatt*, 2 August 2019, https://www.handelsblatt.com/politik/konjunktur/research-institute/geopolitische-analyse-die-unheilvolle-allianz-gegen-die-freiheitliche-weltordnung/24856924.html; and Shaun Walker, 'Syria? Ukraine? Isis? Blame It All On the West's Rampant "Egotism", Putin Says', *Guardian*, 28 September 2015, https://www.theguardian.com/world/2015/sep/28/putin-un-general-assembly-speech.

5   Graf, 'Wahrnehmungen der Bilateralen Beziehungen zu China, Russland und den USA' [Perceptions of Bilateral Relations With China, Russia and the USA] in Steinbrecher et al., *Sicherheits- und verteidigungspolitisches Meinungsbild in der Bundesrepublik Deutschland: Ergebnisse und Analysen der Bevölkerungsbefragung 2020* [Security and Defence Policy Opinions in the Federal Republic of Germany: Results and Analysis of the 2020 Population Survey], pp. 74–89, https://www.bundeswehr.de/resource/blob/5036360/dd413dbbd10610484755c6f4fbfbaa93/download-fober-128-data.pdf.

6   Meia Nouwens and Helena Legarda, 'China's Rise as a Global Security Actor: Implications for NATO', China Security Project, IISS and Mercator Institute for China Studies, December 2020, p. 7, https://www.iiss.org/blogs/research-paper/2020/12/chinas-rise-as-a-global-security-actor; and Jeffrey Mankoff, 'Russian Influence Operations in Germany and Their Effect', Center for Strategic and International Studies, 3 February 2020, https://www.csis.org/analysis/russian-influence-opera-tions-germany-and-their-effect.

7   'Europe's "Sinatra Doctrine" on China', *The Economist*, 11 June 2020, https://www.

economist.com/europe/2020/06/11/
europes-sinatra-doctrine-on-china.

8   Josep Borrell, 'The Sinatra Doctrine: How the EU Should Deal With the US–China Competition', IAI Papers, Istituto Affari Internazionali, 4 September 2020, p. 7, https://www.iai.it/sites/default/files/iaip2024.pdf.

9   In 2018, Germany exported US$110.5bn of goods to China and imported US$126.8bn. See 'World Integrated Trade Solution', World Bank, https://wits.worldbank.org/CountryProfile/en/Country/DEU/Year/LTST/TradeFlow/EXPIMP.

10 Johannes Leithäuser and Michaela Wiegel, 'Was Sich Frankreich und Deutschland von Joe Biden Erhoffen' [What France and Germany Hope for From Joe Biden], *Frankfurter Allgemeine Zeitung*, 26 January 2021, https://www.faz.net/aktuell/politik/von-trump-zu-biden/was-sich-frankreich-und-deutschland-von-biden-erhoffen-17166015.html.

11 Jost Wübbeke et al., 'Made in China 2025: The Making of a High-Tech Superpower and Consequences for Industrial Countries', Mercator Institute for China Studies, 12 August 2016, https://merics.org/en/report/made-china-2025; Zhang Zhihao, 'AI Development Plan Draws Map for Innovation', *China Daily*, 5 August 2019, https://www.chinadaily.com.cn/a/201908/05/WS5d476b48a310cf3e35563d0d.html; and Hideaki Ryugen and Hiroyuki Akiyama, 'China Leads the Way on Global Standards for 5G and Beyond', *Financial Times*, 4 August 2020, https://www.ft.com/content/858d81bd-c42c-404d-b30d-0be32a097f1c.

12 Agatha Kratz et al., 'Chinese FDI in Europe: 2019 Update', Mercator Institute for China Studies, 8 April 2020, https://merics.org/en/report/chinese-fdi-europe-2019-update.

13 Stefan Nicola, 'China's Ping An Buys Stake in German Fintech Incubator Finleap', Bloomberg, 19 November 2018, https://www.bloomberg.com/news/articles/2018-11-19/china-s-ping-an-buys-stake-in-german-fintech-incubator-finleap.

14 Kelly Earley, 'N26 Valued at $3.5bn After $170m Series D Extension', Silicon Republic, 18 July 2019, https://www.siliconrepublic.com/start-ups/n26-value-2019.

15 Jon Russell, 'Alibaba Acquires German Big Data Startup Data Artisans for $103M', *TechCrunch*, 8 January 2019, https://techcrunch.com/2019/01/08/alibaba-data-artisans/.

16 Elsa B. Kania, 'Chinese Military Innovation in Artificial Intelligence', Center for a New American Security, 7 June 2019, https://s3.amazonaws.com/files.cnas.org/documents/June-7-Hearing_Panel-1_Elsa-Kania_Chinese-Military-Innovation-in-Artificial-Intelligence.pdf?mtime=20190617115242.

17 IISS Military Balance+ database, https://milbalplus.iiss.org/, accessed April 2021. The IISS estimates that the total defence expenditure of China is significantly higher than the official defence budget.

18 US Department of Defense, 'Military and Security Developments Involving the People's Republic of China 2020: Annual Report to Congress', September 2020, pp. 24–36, https://media.defense.gov/2020/Sep/01/2002488689/-1/-1/1/2020-dod-china-military-power-report-final.pdf.

19 Richard Haass and David Sacks, 'American Support for Taiwan Must Be Unambiguous', *Foreign Affairs*, 2 September 2020, https://www.foreignaffairs.com/articles/united-states/american-support-taiwan-must-be-unambiguous.

20 Helen Davidson, 'China Could Invade Taiwan in Next Six Years, Top US Admiral

Warns', *Guardian*, 10 March 2021, https://www.theguardian.com/world/2021/mar/10/china-could-invade-taiwan-in-next-six-years-top-us-admiral-warns.

21 Hal Brands, 'What if the U.S. Could Fight Only One War at a Time?', *Japan Times*, 17 June 2019, https://www.japantimes.co.jp/opinion/2019/06/17/commentary/world-commentary/u-s-fight-one-war-time/; Aaron Mehta, 'The US May Not Be Able to Fight Two Big Wars at Once', *Defense News*, 3 October 2018, https://www.defensenews.com/pentagon/2018/10/04/can-the-us-fight-two-big-wars-at-once-new-report-casts-doubts/; Kathy Gilsinan, 'How the U.S. Could Lose a War With China', *Atlantic*, 25 July 2019, https://www.theatlantic.com/politics/archive/2019/07/china-us-war/594793/; Elbridge Colby and David Ochmanek, 'How the United States Could Lose a Great-Power War', *Foreign Policy*, 29 October 2019, https://foreignpolicy.com/2019/10/29/united-states-china-russia-great-power-war/#; and US Senate Committee on Armed Services, 'Confirmation Hearing on the Expected Nomination of Mr. James N. Mattis to Be Secretary of Defense', 12 January 2017, https://www.armed-services.senate.gov/imo/media/doc/17-03_01-12-17.pdf.

22 Nouwens and Legarda, 'China's Rise as a Global Security Actor: Implications for NATO', p. 9. See also Shashank Joshi (@shashj), tweet, 25 February 2021, https://twitter.com/shashj/status/1364924859650875394.

23 See, for example, Barry R. Posen, 'Europe Can Defend Itself', *Survival: Global Politics and Strategy*, vol. 62, no. 6, December 2020–January 2021, pp. 7–34.

24 Pavel K. Baev, 'Russia as Opportunist or Spoiler in the Middle East?', *International Spectator*, vol. 50, no. 2, June 2015, pp. 8–21; Michael Kofman, 'Raiding and International Brigandry: Russia's Strategy for Great Power Competition', War on the Rocks, 14 June 2018, https://warontherocks.com/2018/06/raiding-and-international-brigandry-russias-strategy-for-great-power-competition/; and Julia Gurganus and Eugene Rumer, 'Russia's Global Ambitions in Perspective', Carnegie Endowment for International Peace, 20 February 2019, https://carnegieendowment.org/2019/02/20/russia-s-global-ambitions-in-perspective-pub-78067.

25 Michael Peel, 'EU Envoy Urges Bloc to Engage More With Russia over 5G and Data', *Financial Times*, 13 September 2019, https://www.ft.com/content/725aa5b6-d5f7-11e9-8367-807eb-d53ab77; 'A Thaw in EU–Russia Relations Is Starting: Undeserved Détente', *The Economist*, 12 October 2019, https://www.economist.com/europe/2019/10/12/a-thaw-in-eu-russia-relations-is-starting; Anne-Sylvaine Chassany, 'Macron's Rapprochement With Putin Is Not Worth It', *Financial Times*, 30 September 2020, https://www.ft.com/content/168243c2-bac4-404c-843a-ca1f61196049; and Rym Momtaz, 'Emmanuel Macron's Russian Roulette', Politico, 14 February 2020, https://www.politico.eu/article/emmanuel-macron-russian-roulette-vladimir-putin-security-partner/.

26 See Martin Wight, *Power Politics* (New York: Continuum Books, 1995, reprint), chapter 16; Gordon A. Craig and Alexander L. George, *Force and Statecraft: Diplomatic Problems of Our Time* (Oxford: Oxford University Press, 3rd edition, 1995), chapter 3; and Richard Little, *The Balance of Power in International Relations: Metaphors, Myths and Models* (Cambridge: Cambridge University Press, 2007), chapters 1 and 8.

[27] See IISS, *Russia's Military Modernisation: An Assessment* (Abingdon: Routledge for the IISS, 2020).

[28] Douglas Barrie et al., 'Defending Europe: Scenario-Based Capability Requirements for NATO's European Members', IISS, April 2019, pp. 3, 26–9, 38–41, https://www.iiss.org/blogs/research-paper/2019/05/defending-europe.

[29] Beyond the realm of conventional military capabilities, NATO would also likely have to consider a nuclear asymmetry as it seems plausible that Putin's Russia would at the very least threaten the use of nuclear weapons to dissuade European NATO members from attempting to retake the occupied territory. It is less plausible that NATO would match such an escalation in the scenario discussed here.

[30] Nadège Rolland, 'A China–Russia Condominium Over Eurasia', *Survival: Global Politics and Strategy*, vol. 61, no. 1, February–March 2019, pp. 7–22.

[31] Nouwens and Legarda, 'China's Rise as a Global Security Actor: Implications for NATO', pp. 8–9.

[32] Turkey's status in the DCA arrangement is somewhat unclear. While it is likely that some of its aircraft retain the ability to operate in the nuclear role, US nuclear bombs that used to be designated for use by Turkey have likely been withdrawn from the country.

[33] See, for example, Anthony H. Cordesman, *Deterrence in the 1980s. Part I: American Strategic Forces and Extended Deterrence*, Adelphi Papers, vol. 22, no. 175 (London: International Institute for Strategic Studies, 1982).

[34] Annegret Kramp-Karrenbauer, 'Speech by Federal Minister of Defense Annegret Kramp-Karrenbauer on the Occasion of the Presentation of the Steuben Schurz Media Award on October 23, 2020 in Frankfurt/Main', Bundesministerium der Verteidigung [Federal Ministry of Defence], 23 October 2020, p. 5, https://nato.diplo.de/blob/2409698/75266e6a100b6e35895f431c3ae66c6d/202010 23-rede-akk-medienpreis-data.pdf.

[35] Michael Howard, 'Deterrence, Consensus and Reassurance in the Defence of Europe', in *Defence and Consensus: The Domestic Aspects of Western Security: Part III Papers from the IISS 24th Annual Conference*, Adelphi Papers, vol. 23, no. 184 (London: IISS, 1983), p. 24.

Chapter Five

[1] Lorenz Hemicker, 'Die Lücken der Bundeswehr' [The Gaps in the Bundeswehr], *Frankfurter Allgemeine Zeitung*, 29 April 2020, https://www.faz.net/aktuell/politik/inland/risiko-corona-wachsen-die-luecken-bei-der-bundeswehr-16745947.html.

[2] Lawrence Freedman, 'Does Strategic Studies Have a Future?', in John Baylis, James J. Wirtz and Colin S. Gray (eds), *Strategy in the Contemporary World* (Oxford: Oxford University Press, 6th edition, 2018), p. 418.

[3] Organisation for Economic Co-operation and Development, 'Compare Your Country: Expenditure for Social Purposes', https://www.compareyourcountry.org/social-expenditure/en/0/all/default, accessed 19 March 2021; and John Chipman,

'Shifting weight of military power', IISS Analysis, 29 January 2018, https://www.iiss.org/blogs/analysis/2018/01/shifting-weight.

4   Statistisches Bundesamt [Federal Statistical Office of Germany], 'Volkswirtschaftliche Gesamtrechnungen, Inlandsprodukt' [National Accounts, Domestic Product], https://www.destatis.de/DE/Themen/Wirtschaft/Volkswirtschaftliche-Gesamtrechnungen-Inlandsprodukt/_inhalt.html.

5   Barrie et al., 'Defending Europe: Scenario-Based Capability Requirements for NATO's European Members'.

6   The 80/20 split represents a middle ground of estimates. See Andrés Navarro-Galera, Rodrigo I. Ortúzar-Maturana and Francisco Muñoz-Leiva, 'The Application of Life Cycle Costing in Evaluating Military Investments: An Empirical Study at an International Scale', Defence and Peace Economics, vol. 22, no. 5, 2011, pp. 509–43.

7   Deutscher Bundestag [German Bundestag], 'Unterrichtung durch die Wehrbeauftragte' [Briefing By the Armed Forces Commissioner], Jahresbericht 2020 (62. Bericht) [Annual Report 2020 (62nd Report)], Drucksache 19/26600 [Printed Matter 19/26600], 23 February 2021, pp. 82–92, https://dip21.bundestag.de/dip21/btd/19/266/1926600.pdf.

8   Martin Sebaldt, 'Rüstungspolitik im Zeichen des Versagens: Die Trendwende Material der Bundeswehr Zwischen Anspruch und Realität' [Armament Policy in Decay: The Equipment Turnaround of the German Bundeswehr Between Aspiration and Reality], Zeitschrift für Außen- und Sicherheitspolitik, vol. 13, no. 2, June 2020, pp. 177–96, especially p. 179.

9   Franz-Stefan Gady, 'What Does AI Mean for the Future of Manoeuvre Warfare?', IISS, 5 May 2020, https://www.iiss.org/blogs/analysis/2020/05/csfc-ai-manoeuvre-warfare.

10   See François Heisbourg and Maximilian Terhalle, '6 Post-Cold War Taboos Europe Must Now Face', Politico, 28 December 2018, https://www.politico.eu/article/6-post-cold-war-taboos-europe-must-now-face-merkel-macron-trump-nato-eurozone-reform/; François Heisbourg, 'Europe Can Afford the Cost of Autonomy', Survival: Global Politics and Strategy, vol. 63, no. 1, February–March 2021, pp. 25–32, especially pp. 28–9; and Barrie and Giegerich, 'Berlin and the Bomb'. See also Richard Barrons and Maximilian Terhalle, 'Europe Needs to Calculate for the U.S. Military's Shortcomings', National Interest, 6 August 2019, https://nationalinterest.org/feature/europe-needs-calculate-us-militarys-shortcomings-71756; Klaus Naumann and Maximilian Terhalle, 'Deutschlands Schlafwandeln gefährdet die liberale Weltordnung' [Germany's Sleepwalking Endangers the Liberal World Order], Die Welt, 26 November 2019, https://www.welt.de/debatte/kommentare/plus203825868/Nato-Deutschlands-Schlafwandeln-gefaehrdet-die-liberale-Weltordnung.html; and Maximilian Terhalle, 'Europas Augenblick ist gekommen' [Europe's Moment Has Come], Frankfurter Allgemeine Zeitung, 15 February 2018, https://www.faz.net/aktuell/politik/sicherheitskonferenz/gastbeitrag-eine-strategische-vision-fuer-europa-15446611.html. It is possible that making French missiles available to German aircraft could further complicate the airframe selection for the Tornado replacement in Germany.

11 Bastian Giegerich and Alexandra Jonas, 'Auf der Suche Nach Best Practice? Die Entstehung Nationaler Sicherheitsstrategien im Internationalen Vergleich' [Searching For Best Practice? The Development of National Security Strategies in an International Comparison], *Sicherheit und Frieden*, vol. 30, no. 3, 2012, pp. 129–34.

INDEX

Adelphi books are published six times a year by Routledge Journals, an imprint of Taylor & Francis, 4 Park Square, Milton Park, Abingdon, Oxfordshire OX14 4RN, UK.

A subscription to the institution print edition, ISSN 1944-5571, includes free access for any number of concurrent users across a local area network to the online edition, ISSN 1944-558X. Taylor & Francis has a flexible approach to subscriptions enabling us to match individual libraries' requirements. This journal is available via a traditional institutional subscription (either print with free online access, or online-only at a discount) or as part of our libraries, subject collections or archives. For more information on our sales packages please visit www.tandfonline.com/page/librarians.

2021 Annual Adelphi Subscription Rates			
Institution	£881	US$1,629	€1,304
Individual	£302	US$517	€413
Online only	£749	US$1,314	€1,108

Dollar rates apply to subscribers outside Europe. Euro rates apply to all subscribers in Europe except the UK and the Republic of Ireland where the pound sterling price applies. All subscriptions are payable in advance and all rates include postage. Journals are sent by air to the USA, Canada, Mexico, India, Japan and Australasia. Subscriptions are entered on an annual basis, i.e. January to December. Payment may be made by sterling cheque, dollar cheque, international money order, National Giro, or credit card (Amex, Visa, Mastercard).

For a complete and up-to-date guide to Taylor & Francis journals and books publishing programmes, and details of advertising in our journals, visit our website: **http://www.tandfonline.com.**

Ordering information:
USA/Canada: Taylor & Francis Inc., Journals Department, 530 Walnut Street, Suite 850, Philadelphia, PA 19106, USA. **UK/Europe/Rest of World:** Routledge Journals, T&F Customer Services, T&F Informa UK Ltd., Sheepen Place, Colchester, Essex, CO3 3LP, UK.

Advertising enquiries to:
USA/Canada: The Advertising Manager, Taylor & Francis Inc., 530 Walnut Street, Suite 850, Philadelphia, PA 19106, USA. Tel: +1 (800) 354 1420. Fax: +1 (215) 207 0050. **UK/Europe/Rest of World**: The Advertising Manager, Routledge Journals, Taylor & Francis, 4 Park Square, Milton Park, Abingdon, Oxfordshire OX14 4RN, UK. Tel: +44 (0) 20 7017 6000. Fax: +44 (0) 20 7017 6336.